THE PIECES COME TOGETHER

- AT LAST -

The Memoirs of an Adult Adoptee

And her Sister

By

Patricia A. Walsh

Arlene Patricia Loucks

**The Pieces Come Together…at Last:
The Memoirs of an Adult Adoptee and Her Sister**

Copyright © 2013 by Panda Books, Schenectady, NY
ISBN: 978-1484806340

All rights reserved. Printed in the United States of America.
No part of this book may be reproduced
in any manner without permission.

Dedicated to
Our Mother
Elizabeth "Betty" Morris Richter
With Our Love

Prologue:

Times of surprise and times of joy enter our lives in strange ways. Our story chronicles just such times that have been experienced by two mature adult women, when their lives became woven together in an amazing way.

As friends and family heard of our odyssey, many suggested that we share it with others. They felt that it might be a source of encouragement for those seeking to know their ancestry.

It would also serve as a story with a happy ending, which we so much need in today's world.

Our story is told in two voices. Each, speaking for herself, will reveal her separate life, her thoughts as we unlocked the mystery, and her individual reactions to the various stages in this journey.

Together we will tell how we are exploring our common interests, establishing our own "traditions," and becoming friends.

The names of some family members have been changed, honoring their request that we do so.

We owe a tremendous debt of gratitude to:

   ... Sarah McCall and her son, Michael,

     for helping to bring about our meeting,

        ... our families who have shared our joy

           ... our friends who have suggested and

              supported the writing of this memoir.

Forward

<u>Roots</u> started a trend. All of the world suddenly began to search the fertile ground from whence they sprang, were nurtured and then passed along the basic traits and rituals that belonged, uniquely, to that family.

There are those of us who will never know what made us to be the person that people see – a blond, a brunette, a blue-eyed fair skinned girl or a dark haired olive skinned boy. But we will always know and love the family which molded and shaped, chiseled and caressed us into the person we have become.

In one relative's account of our family history, I was "acquired." In another version, by a more sensitive aunt, my parents were the object of pity as they "with barely adequate means, took on a child to raise as their own." Be those observations as they may, one outside the situation can never assess the hearts and minds that made that heroic decision. It was truly a leap of faith and love.

I have never doubted for an instant that I was loved with all the love a parent's heart could hold and more love than their Irish Catholic roots would permit display.

While I was never "driven" to find my birth family, I was always curious. I found myself fashioning scenarios in my mind. As I matured the curiosity took many forms. More questions arose. Health history became a crucial aspect of my need to begin a search. Soon, I knew that I would have to take the small pieces of information that I had and try to piece them into enough solid data that I could follow the trail. I knew that the attempts I made might not yield the fruit for which I had hoped. I knew that members of my birth family might not be willing to welcome this stranger of nearly 70 years into a solid, existing family. Yet I could not deny myself the *possibility* that I could find answers to some of my questions.

And so it was that I took the giant step of beginning my search. Where does one begin? The internet seemed to be the most logical place to begin. Technology had made available records from many sources. These were very well organized and accessible through the web site of the Church of Jesus Christ of Latter Day Saints (The Mormons).

In putting this memoir together, it is my hope that someone who is in a similar situation may find the courage to begin to find their missing pieces. There is a television show which focuses on "reunions" with missing family members. The slogan that begins each episode states it so well: *You can not find peace until you find all the pieces.* Ironically, I had selected the title of my search, <u>*The Pieces Come Together . . . at Last*</u>, before the television show began. The search is so akin to putting a puzzle together piece by piece. You set a piece aside until its place becomes obvious. You match the parts that create an image. You take a break from the challenge and return to it with renewed determination.

In recounting our story from my adoption to the inexpressible joy of finding and becoming a part of my birth family, I hope that you will enjoy the journey with us. If it is a springboard for your own search, may you have an outcome that will bring you peace of mind and heart whether or not it brings answers to all of your questions.

P at

If you are an older child in a family, perhaps you remember the anticipation of your sibling's arrival. If you are old enough, it is most likely that the time of expectation was not known to you. It may have come as a complete surprise to you when this new little person, not only came to your house, but *stayed*. From that moment on, your life changed forever. I was nearly 11 when my little sister was born. But it would be several years before the full impact of her birth came to me. Several years can be numbered at 57 until I was aware that I had a sister. It wasn't until she was approaching her 59th birthday and I was nearly 70 that I met my little sister.

No matter the years, my life was joyfully changed forever when my little sister, Arlene, came into my life and I met her for the first time.

A rlene

I hope this story will help to give others hope – hope of finding that "missing piece" of their own puzzle

– and the courage to take that first step. I wasn't the one taking that first step, but I'm sure it can be daunting, it can be scary to be sure, but it *can* turn out to be something beautiful! Not all "missing pieces" *don't* want to be found! It certainly has changed my life – and changed it for the better!

P   Let me take you on the journey that brought me to this point.

From my earliest days, as a very small child, I knew that I was adopted. This was a part of who I was. It was not an anomaly, but it was my reality. Since it was not a fact that was discussed or referred to in gatherings of our extended family, I was never sure of who among my cousins knew. This was not important to me throughout the years.

My nurturing family was large and close. I was raised as an only child, but I had four first cousins on my father's side of the family and nine on my mother's side. In the childhood days of my life many of these cousins were living within our small village of Scotia, NY and others were within a 10 mile radius. Then, of course, there were second cousins. I literally had cousins by the dozens. Perhaps it was because I was an only child, that my cousins were so important to me. Seeing these relatives was a regular and happy part of my early life

Holidays and birthdays were always times for gathering the family together. Being with my cousins was always fun for me. During many summers in the late 1940's, my cousins Elizabeth, Barbara and Peter would journey from their homes in Brooklyn, and then White Plains, and spend a couple of weeks at our home. Their parents, my Aunt Mary and Uncle Frank, would leave them with my parents and travel on to Montreal for a vacation. What fun it was to have them around for an extended period of time. Many days would be spent with our cousins, Raymond and Gail, who lived mere blocks from our house. Evening treats on those hot summer nights would include getting into our pajamas and piling into the car. We'd head for the locks on the Mohawk River and watch the boats pass through. A favorite daytime excursion was to a local pony farm for rides. It seemed that these special treats were reserved for times when the cousins were here. No wonder I loved having them around, missed them when they left for home and looked forward to their next visit.

A I grew up an only child in a very small family. I had only two cousins, Ted, in Trumbull, Connecticut, and Dotty, in Hudson Falls, New York. My father had been married before and had 2 children, Walt, Jr. (Bud), and Betty (yes, Bud and Betty, just like the Andersons on Father Knows Best – does anyone still remember that?). They both grew up in Connecticut and, by the time I came along, Bud was 17 years old and Betty was 11. I vaguely remember Bud marrying Angie and their daughter, Debbie, was born when I was 5 years old. The only times I would see Bud were usually during the summer at our grandparents' house in Waterbury, Connecticut. Although I may have only seen Bud a few times a year, I idolized him! He always took time for me, always paid attention to me. After I'd get bored hanging out with the adults, I would usually wander away to play with my toys. Bud would always find me and join in playing dolls or playing office. Everyone always said where you found one, you found the other. I was SO proud that he was my brother.

One of the happiest memories I have was at my cousin, Ted's, wedding in 1965. During the reception, my brother, my mother and I were sitting at our table and my brother asked if I would like to spend my Christmas vacation at his house. Of course I said yes! My mother asked if maybe he should ask Angie first and his reply was, "Angie's only my wife. Arlene's my sister."

Unfortunately, I didn't have any kind of relationship with Betty. In fact, I had never even seen Bud and Betty together. I would only see her when my parents and I would go to her house in Danbury, Ct., which didn't happen very often. The one and only time she and her husband showed up at one of the get-togethers at our grandparents' house, Bud didn't show up. After several unanswered phone calls to Bud's house, my grandmother made a call to Angie's sister and was told they "went on a picnic." There was something definitely going on there that I didn't understand at the time, nor do I understand it now, but some kind of "dysfunction" was happening. When I married in 1968, along with her wedding gift, Betty sent me a letter saying that what had happened between our father and her had nothing to do with my mother or me and, now that I was older, maybe I would understand. Well, I'm *way* older now and I still don't. I regret not contacting her at that time. It may have been that I was so young. I was technically an adult – I was getting married after all – but I was only 18. I really wish I had handled it differently. My father passed away in 1975, my brother passed away in 1976 and, when my mother passed away in 1977, I had no further contact with my sister at all. I always felt badly about that.

All my friends had brothers and/or sisters and they were a little jealous of me for being an only child. I didn't understand that at all! If your parents made you go with them for a visit to relatives or just for a Sunday drive, you had your sibling; I had my dolls.

It may sound strange to those with siblings, but I feel I "missed out" because I never had anyone to argue with. I also feel this contributed to the fact that I absolutely hate confrontation. My parents never argued – well, they did, but never with any yelling or derogatory comments. They could be a little "snarky" from time to time but, in general, they were always very "civilized." As a result, if I'm around people who are arguing or if, heaven forbid, someone yells at me, I have a very hard time handling it. And I wonder if other "onlies" have that problem. I must ask my sister.

One night, when I was about 8 years old, I remember crying – REALLY crying – and begging my mother for a brother or a sister. I didn't care which, just a sibling. She sort of laughed and told me she was too old for that. I suggested we could adopt – I had it all figured out. Looking back, I can't imagine how that made her feel. Her only comment about adoption was that it was too expensive.

P In 1950, (the year Arlene was born) when I was 11 years old, my family took a wonderful trip. Traveling by car, we crossed the country to visit my mother's brother, Edward, in Glendale, CA, just outside of Los Angeles. This trip was long and at times seemed neigh on to endless. I don't remember ever asking the famous question: "Are we there yet?" There was so much to see. It seemed as if every day we were "there." And I just had to spot a Dairy Queen so that we could stop for a break and a treat. The DQ chain had not yet reached the East coast, so the novelty was doubly exciting. We saw unbelievable sights and

13

suddenly "geography" became real to me. On several occasions we stopped at State or National parks. We'd pitch our tent, make supper and travel throughout the park. Seeing geysers at Yellowstone, sky high waterfalls in Yosemite, the towering mountain peaks of Glacier National Park and the unbelievable beauty of the Grand Canyon, was an experience of a lifetime, at least of my young lifetime. To this day those images are vivid in my memory. My parents had camped often in their younger days. As I was introduced to the exciting lifestyle of a camper, I grew to love it. I loved meeting the other children at the campsites. I loved the adventures offered by the camp rangers. I went horse back riding at Glacier and Yosemite National Parks and at the Grand Canyon. In mid July, we climbed snow banks in Yellowstone Park. We wandered the rugged hillside along the road through the Black Hills of South Dakota.

One evening as my father and I slept in our tent at Yellowstone Park, my mother was frightened, but too afraid to make a sound. As she reported the incident in the morning, there had been the large silhouette of a bear outlined on the wall of the tent. How close the creature was, was hard to tell. But in the moonlight, she said it looked immense. Fortunately, we had followed the ranger's directive and had secured all food in the car. Apparently, without food available to him, our campsite was not all that interesting. He (or she) wandered off and posed no threat to us. Our brief stay at each park was packed with excitement and we continued on our way with memories that have lasted to this day.

During the week at the home of my uncle in Los Angeles, we traveled to Tiajuana, Mexico, saw the hand and foot prints of the stars at Grauman's Chinese Theater, went horseback riding at Griffith Park and had my silhouette hand-cut at an artist's booth on Olvera Street.

It was a wonderful way to spend a childhood summer and surely made a good topic for the first assignment of the school year, "How I spent My Summer Vacation."

As I grew up, our vacations were taken a bit closer to home. I had been as far north as Moosehead Lake, Maine, and as far south as Richmond, Virginia. The trip to Virginia was to visit a cousin of my mother's and included a stop in Washington, D.C., which this cousin told us, for our own sanity, we should avoid during rush hour. So, of course, that's precisely when we arrived. But no matter, we saw the White House, toured the Capitol building, saw the Lincoln Memorial and Washington Monument. My mother had taken some amazing photos inside the Capitol, especially in the Hall of Presidents and the rotunda. Unfortunately, this was back before digital cameras, when you had to let the "professionals" handle the development of the photos and these had been ruined in the process but, on the bright side, we got a couple free rolls of film, so I guess that made us even.

Some of our other trips had been through Massachusetts (Plymouth, Concord, Gloucester – do NOT go to Gloucester - or any seaside fishing village for that matter - at low tide), Vermont, New Hampshire. All so beautiful and so rich in history.

But the most memorable trip occurred when I was around 10 years old. My parents decided that we should join my aunt and uncle on a camping trip to Canada. My cousin, Dotty, was about 19 years old, had a job and had to stay home. Lucky her! She loaded me up with movie magazines and comic books while my aunt sent list upon list to my mother of all the necessary camping supplies. This planning took an entire year! I'm sure my parents were sick of the whole thing before we even pulled out of the driveway! The day finally came and we headed for Hudson Falls to meet up with my aunt and uncle, then off we go, following their converted school bus. The drive to Canada was uneventful until we were going through Customs. Everyone had birth certificates, which was all that was needed at the time, the agent asked a few questions and, just as my father was putting his window up, the alarm clock, waaaay in the back of our station wagon, started going off! If that happened today, I'd hate the think what would happen!

We continued driving....and continued driving....and continued driving. FINALLY, we pulled into a camping ground. There is absolutely nothing around but trees. They said there was a lake there, but I sure couldn't see it. We pulled our rented tent out of the car and started to put it up. We had all the poles to hold up the tent, but no stakes and no ropes. Wonderful. My mother and father went looking for tree branches to use for stakes and, naturally, my aunt and uncle had extra rope. As they were putting the poles in the proper places, we noticed a rip between the floor and one wall of the tent. A FOURTEEN FOOT rip! As luck would have it, again, my aunt was fully prepared for any contingency and happened to have, oh, maybe a MILLION safety pins and she and my mother spent I don't know HOW long pinning the tent together! Even at 10 years old, I already knew this is going to be SO fun!

This trip was supposed to be 2 weeks of fun, sun, fishing and swimming. Right. How about rain EVERY day – EVERY DAY! My aunt and uncle were snug and warm in their heated bus, cooking on a stove, while we sat in the damp tent cooking over charcoal. One day, my father asked my uncle to go fishing and they left fairly early. A couple hours later, my mother and I went to see what my aunt was up to and what a mistake THAT was! She was absolutely furious! How dare my father ask my uncle to go fishing and NOT ask her. She further informed us that she was not used to being ignored. We slunk back to our tent and sat inside (because of the rain) until the men came back. You can believe my father got an earful when he got back. What was he thinking?

Everyone eventually got over being angry and we now did everything TOGETHER. Like take a drive to the dump – TO THE DUMP – to look at the bears. As a 10-year-old kid, I don't have to tell you how excited I was with THAT trip. One day we took the 90-mile drive to the closest town, which consisted of two churches, a diner with general store and a gas station. I do have to mention that, on the drive back to camp, we saw a double rainbow (the first I had ever seen) and a moose (also the first – and only-one I've ever seen) and it was the first and only time I'd ever seen the very beautiful, yet very strange and very scary, aurora borealis.

Evenings were spent in the bus with the adults playing cards and me reading. Did I mention we brought our dog? He kept getting tangled up around the poles in the bus and I repeatedly had to free him. I must have sighed too loudly because my aunt commented that she knew SOMEONE who wasn't having a good time. Really? You think? At that point, my father informed her that I was doing better than HE was and it was, after only 1 week, time to go. YIPEE!!!!

That night we had the worst thunder storm I have ever experienced. And we were in a TENT. With metal poles. AND a fourteen-foot rip. When it finally subsided a bit, my mother asked, "Is anyone awake?" Are you kidding?

We were all awake, just too scared to talk! Since we were perched on top of a hill, we were all waiting to be washed down it, into the woods. We all jumped up at the same time and started packing. My aunt and uncle had planned on staying, but, for whatever reason, decided to leave with us.

The really eventful (for me) part of this trip happened that evening. By 7pm or so, all 3 of us were starving and we pulled into a diner, with my aunt and uncle pulling in behind us. No matter what this diner served, we would have gobbled it up and enjoyed it completely. My aunt, however, was not impressed and made no effort to hide this fact. By this time, my mother was in tears and I didn't take too kindly to that. When we got outside, they got into their bus and I just snapped. I stood in front of their open bus door, started crying and screaming "I hate you" over and over again at the top of my lungs! I'm sure my parents were horrified as they shuffled me off to our car, but I sure did feel better! The only other part of that trip I remember is staying in a motel that night. With a real bed!

It took several months before there was any kind of correspondence between my parents and my aunt and uncle. I can't imagine how hard it must have been. After your child screams in someone's face that she hates them, what do you say? "She was tired – you know how she gets when she's tired." Yes, that must have been it – tired – and cranky. Apparently.

I have been on subsequent camping trips with my husband and children. For a few years in a row, we would spend a week in June at a nearby lake in upstate New York – in a small camping trailer – no tent. We didn't always have great weather – I have a picture of our raft floating in a huge puddle in front of our camper – but we always had fun. My kids had the choice of swimming and sunning with me or fishing with their Dad during the day. In the evenings, they met some other kids in the area, a couple of whom lived on a houseboat year-round. Back then, gas was a bit cheaper and friends would drive up after work to grill hotdogs and hamburgers. These were definitely better experiences, even if it rained, although I'm still not all that fond of it. However, I think I would try it again.

P My four cousins on my father's side of the family lived in Scotia. Their ages did not make them playmates for me. But they were very much a part of my life. The younger ones provided me with a wonderful opportunity to babysit. Many nights I would let Kathy and Joey stay up until I heard the car in the driveway and then we'd all dive into our beds and be "sound asleep" when my aunt and uncle came into the house. I'm sure they were on to our scheme, but they never said anything about it to me.

When Joey was a year and a half old, he broke his leg. The little tyke was in an awkward traction unit in his crib. I think it was more uncomfortable for the rest of us watching him than it was for Joey. Each day, after school, I would go down to their house and play with him. He laughed easily and had a winning smile all the time. Many times when he was being a bit of a challenge for my aunt, she would say to me, "You can have him for a nickel." Although I brought her the nickel, she never relinquished him. After six weeks flat on his back, Joey had a cute little bald spot on the back of his head.

Throughout the years many people have said that growing up as an only child, I must have been spoiled. I beg to differ with that stereotype. I was raised with the Three R's: rules, regulations, and responsibilities. Helping at home was expected. Drying dishes, dusting furniture, ironing and folding laundry were regular chores. Doing homework was demanded before any other activities each evening of the school year. I'm not saying that I was always happy about these duties. It would have been nice to have siblings with whom I could share the jobs. I did not get everything that I wanted. I begged my parents for a horse. There was never a horse in our yard. I always wanted an electric train. My father said, "You're a girl and girls don't play with trains." End of story. Much as I wanted to say, "But if I had one, I'd play with it," I knew better and I held my tongue. So it is quite fair to say that I was not spoiled as a child. And from the other "only child" people that I have known, this was quite typical.

There was one brief period in my life when I had to share the attention of my parents with another child. Due to a family illness, my parents offered to take in a three-year-old cousin for the duration of her mother's recuperation. So for about nine months, I had to share my toys with Honey. Since I was six years old at the time, I was off to school each day. Honey could stay home with my mother. Somehow that didn't seem fair to me. But upon my arrival home each day, I would play school with her and teach her what I had learned. We had fun together, sometimes. It was not so much fun when she was allowed to rip the bandage off my scraped knee. But it made her laugh and keeping this little visitor happy was what we seemed to be all about. After all, she was away from her mother and father. Each weekend Honey's parents would come to visit her. Happily, in later life, I learned that she had no recollection of that traumatic period in my life. It had obviously served the purpose of having her in a safe and loving place until she could be reunited with her parents and her older sister.

A When I had my first child, Gwen, in 1971, I knew I had to have at least one more. I could *not* let her be an only child. My second daughter, Kristine, was born in 1975. One of the ways Gwen used to torture her sister was by telling her, in a very wistful voice, "I remember when *I* was an only child. I used to get EVERYTHING I wanted." Not true. Where do people get the idea that only children are spoiled? Probably from people like my daughter – who LIE!

Like I said, I had a very small family. My only 2 cousins, Ted and Dotty, were a bit older than I was, so we never had what you would call a close relationship. I saw Dotty quite often growing up and some of my best memories are of Christmas in Hudson Falls with Dotty and all her friends, playing records and dancing. Age differences don't matter much as you get older, but I had long since lost contact with both my cousins. I found out from Michael that Dotty passed away in 2002. Very sad.

P As we grew up, many of the cousins moved away from the area. Uncle Harry moved to Marblehead, Massachusetts in response to a job transfer to the General Electric Company in Lynn, MA. That took our three oldest cousins and their younger brother out of our immediate area. In the late 1950's, as Raymond and I were at the end of our high school years, his dad was transferred to the GE Plant in Binghamton. NY. And thus my lifelong playmate and friend moved away. By now we were young adults and headed to college.

The years of my childhood were peopled by those who loved me. The memories of our times together are happy ones. Our frequent travels to visit the family kept us close in spite of the miles that had come between us.

As these families moved away, I remained in the locale of origin for our ancestors. When genealogy became a passionate focus for three of us, I had the advantage of having known many of the "old folks." I was familiar with the towns and villages of our history and knew, quite well, the cemeteries where our ancestors were buried. Truly, this was MY family and I was one of them. I was one of them in every aspect of my life. Or so it seemed.

The fair skinned, blue-eyed cousins all resembled each other. My olive skin, straight hair and brown eyes had no match in the family circle. As I grew up, I quickly towered over my Mother and Father. I cannot count the number of times casual acquaintances would say, "Where did you get your height? You must be adopted." I never responded to these quips with other than a shrug of the shoulders.

Meeting of Adoptees

At an early point in my quest to find resources that could possibly lead to garnering some information on my birth family, I saw the notice of a meeting to be held at a local library. It stated that the gathering would be specifically for adult adoptees. It seemed to be an opportunity to share the experience of being an adopted child, grown to adulthood. It was my assumption that there would be a further discussion of the tools available to do research. It is a firm law that, in New York State, adoptions dating back to the time of my infancy, all records of the identities of the birth family would be sealed. This carried the reverse assurance that the adoptive family would remain anonymous, thus preventing any contact or outreach or intrusion by either party.

It must be stated at this point that throughout the years of my childhood, rebellion against my family was never an issue. I was aware of my status in the family. By virtue of the legal process of adoption, I was the child of John and Marguerite. I was truly loved by them. I was cared for by them. I was raised in a home that was characterized by discipline and expectations of work and study. In short, I was reared with no reference being made to being anything other than their child. In turn, it was never my habit to make a disparaging reference by statements such as, "You're not my real mother/father."

This being said, all this came as a shock to me as I listened to the conversation at the Library on that Saturday morning. The tone of each person was that of anger. Their focus was the fact that they had been "thrown away." They sought explanations of, "Why?" They each spoke of their *right* to know their background. The longer the meeting went on, the more uneasy I became. I made a few attempts to offer a possible rationale for the unanswered questions in their lives.

Perhaps my attitude toward my own adoption was a result of the explanation given to me from my earliest remembrance. I was told that a young girl was not in a position to be the Mother to a baby at the time I was born. Through the years, I conjured up in my mind, possible scenarios. But no matter the story I created, the bottom line was always that my birth mother had to make a very difficult choice. She courageously made that decision, knowing that she would never see the child to whom she had given the gift of life. Unselfishly, she took the steps necessary to ensure that her baby girl would have parents who wanted a child to love. This child they would willingly take into their home and raise with unquestioning and unconditional love.

There is no way for me to know the pain that it may have caused my birth mother when she relinquished her parental rights. I do not know if it was completely her choice, or if she was led to the decision by those around her. No matter the motivation, she deserved the option of beginning her life anew, knowing that she had done the right thing for that time and situation, taking into consideration her baby and herself.

An accurate and updated medical history would be of great advantage. This is a possibility these days, through the NYS Adoption Registry. These records with non-identifying information can be obtained. Their accuracy is dependent upon the birth parents fidelity to keeping the information current as significant medical events occur in their lives. This resource was of no use to me, because the most current information contained in the Adoption Registry was entered in June of 1939 when the final papers were signed, releasing me for adoption.

Any of this dialogue was not what these people wanted to hear that Saturday morning. They were firmly entrenched in their anger and frustration. At one point a woman made a remark which was said in an accusatory tone. "You sound more like a birth mother than an adoptee." If she meant that as an insult she missed her mark, for to me it sounded like a compliment. I was being identified with a woman of courage, compassion and right judgment in the face of a heart wrenching decision.

 So let us fast-forward to February of 2007.

Having pretty well exhausted the genealogy research available to us, my cousins and I had come to the end of our task. Since the 1930 US Federal Census was released after 2002, I decided to take the little information that I had and see if I could get any information on the family of my birth. That would be the family that gave me the height, hair and eyes that had separated me from the family into which I had been lovingly inserted and unconditionally accepted.

Since all adoption information in New York State was, and to this day is, sealed, I do not know where the information had come from. The facts that I had, had been a part of my knowledge reserve for as long as I could remember. I was born at Saint Joseph's Maternity Hospital, a home for unwed mothers in Troy, NY. My name was Patricia Ann Morris. My birth mother's name was Elizabeth and she had come from a small town in upstate New York. Armed with this limited knowledge, I combed the census reports from three small towns from which I believed Elizabeth may have come. I have no recollection of the source of this information, only that my mother had made reference to the name and location on a few occasions.

It was not long until I found a young girl of 10 named, Elizabeth Morris living with her mother and brother. If, as the census recorded, she was 10 in 1930, she would be 19 in 1939, the year of my birth. This was the closest I had come to finding a person who could have been my birth mother. On the website that I was using, there was a notation of "others looking for Elizabeth Morris," along with a contact option. What was there to lose? It was worth a try. It was a wild shot that has made all the difference.

Based on that window of opportunity, on February 27, 2007 I sent an e-mail directly through Ancestry.com to that *other* person.

Citing the entry that I had found on Ancestry.com, I asked

2/27/2007

"Do you have more information about this person that you could share with me? I would be interested to know if that is a married or maiden name. I am looking for an Elizabeth Morris who resided in the Glens Falls/HudsonFalls/Fort Edward area in the late 1930's. Thank You"

On the same evening I received a response, again through Ancestry.com. They ensure that all contact is anonymous until the time comes when the two parties determine that it is appropriate and safe to make direct contact.

Wisely, I was asked why I was interested in Elizabeth.

2/27/2007

"Hello, This Elizabeth Morris is my second cousin on my mother's side. Morris is her maiden name, . Betty died in 1977. She had a brother who also passed away. I think Betty was living in South Glens Falls in the 1930's They lived in Maine for a time, her father died in a work related accident at the International Paper Mill in 1927. If you think this is the Betty Morris you're looking for please get back in touch with me. The Betty Morris you are looking for; how are you related?"

This was a question to which an answer was definitely in order.

2/27/2007

"Thank you for such a speedy response to my inquiry. I do not know if this ELIZABETH MORRIS is related. But she seemed to match the little information that I had. As a cousin, you may not have the information I am looking for. Actually, I am looking for my birth mother. I was adopted as an infant. I have no intention of disrupting a family, but am curious about the health history that is a part of my background. I had always thought about the circumstances which might have led a young woman to have the courage to seek a home for a child she was not prepared to care for. I had a wonderful childhood in a loving family and would in no way want to upset a family that perhaps, had no knowledge of another child. If in fact you know if this is a possibility, I would appreciate further communication on the subject. I must say that I am sorry to hear that this Elizabeth Morris died in 1977- still quite a young woman of 57. Again, thank you for your reply."

Having clarified my intentions in my search, I was elated to receive this message the following day.

2/28/2007

"First of all my name is Michael. I was very overwhelmed by your e-mail. I have been researching my family tree for close to five years...Now, I'm fairly sure we are cousins. I talked to my mother (my mother and Betty were both born in 1920) and she told me I should respond to your e-mail. I'm trying to ease into this as gently as I can, but yes Betty had a child out of wedlock...She went to Troy, NY to have the baby around 1940. I would guess it was a home for unwed mothers. My mother couldn't think of the name of the father, but he refused to marry Betty...

Betty settled down and married a gentleman ... and they lived for about 28 years in Schenectady, NY. They had one daughter together and the daughter had two children. Betty's obituary states she died unexpectedly at her Schenectady home...after a short illness at the age of 57....

I'm going to give you my e-mail address and hope to hear back from you...Regards, Mike"

2/28/2007

Hello Michael,

You cannot know how wonderful it feels to have some answers to questions that are as old as I am. Yes, I was born in Troy, NY at St. Joseph's Maternity Hospital in March 1939 and remained in the care of the Sisters of St. Joseph there, until my adoption in December of 1939.

I have long tried to find a way to find the family of my birth, but did not feel that it was fair to my parents to do it until after their deaths. My mother died in 1990 and I have been searching census files, etc. ever since. Now that the 1930 census has been released, the door has opened. My greatest regret is that I never had the opportunity to thank Betty for giving me LIFE and a wonderful life with a childless couple with the desire to share their love with a child.

I have often dreamed of meeting someone who might look like me. A silly dream, I realize.

How ironic that Betty lived in Schenectady for 28 years. I wonder what part of Schenectady. I grew up in Scotia and to this day, live in the house of my childhood. I may have passed her on the street and never known that we had a connection.

I would love to have any information – names, dates, pictures, obituary notice – of the family of Elizabeth that you feel could be shared without offending anyone involved. Thank your mother for me, for encouraging you to respond to my e-mail. I was afraid that perhaps it was a situation that was lost in passing down the family stories.

My head and heart are still somewhere between unbounded joy and deep peace.

Thank you again for finding the missing pieces of my life-puzzle.   Pat

At this point we began a two year correspondence, e-mailing directly without the filter of Ancestry.com.

The gentleman, Michael McCall, who responded, opened a door that would bring me, without a doubt, to the family I had been seeking. Michael corroborated the information with his Mother, Sarah, who was the first cousin to Elizabeth. They had grown up together and she was aware of the fact that her cousin had gone to Troy to have a baby. Our correspondence had brought the sad information that my birth mother had died nearly 30 years earlier at the age of 57. Now I was beginning to glean some other important information that I had been looking for - medical history. Emotions began to surface. The questions that I never realized that I wanted answered were spilling out and awaiting response.

3/1/2007

"Good Morning, Michael,

I am still reeling from the events that are unfolding!

I have one other question that has long been of interest (concern) to me.

I was raised in a close-knit Irish Catholic family, but I bear no resemblance to them of course. My curiosity is the national heritage of my family of birth. Since all of my cousins are small of stature, blue-eyed and fair skinned and I am tall, brown-eyed and olive skinned, I don't feel that Ireland is a primary factor of my genetic make-up. Because of the years I have spent being Irish, it will always be a part of me.

You mentioned that Betty had worked as a waitress at the Carl Company...I went to school in downtown Schenectady (St. Joseph's Academy). I spent many noon hours at the Carl Company, even occasionally grabbing a quick lunch at the little dinette counter there in the mid to late 50's. What a small world! Pat"

The amazing thing in this whole research process was

31

finding that Elizabeth had moved to Schenectady in the early 1950's with her new husband and their small baby. Schenectady was the city where I attended Saint Joseph's Academy from fourth grade through high school graduation. Although I lived in the neighboring village of Scotia, Schenectady was where my parent's families had lived. It was where many of my cousins lived. It was where we shopped in the large department stores – Wallace's, Barney's and The Carl Company. Little did I know as I shopped at The Carl Company, that my birth mother was employed there. Did I ever see her? Would she have recognized me? Was she even aware that she had moved her young family to the area where her other child lived? These questions have haunted me since those pieces of her life have been revealed to me.

Michael's response to my question about national origin came as quite a surprise. It brought a revelation that I had not expected.

3/1/2007

Hi, Pat,

Please, you may ask as many questions as you like. I know I would. If I can answer them, I will.

Well, the Irish Heritage is a part of your birth mother's family. Betty's grandmother, her father's mother, Mary McClosky Morris, was Irish/Canadian. Her dad, John was born in Ireland and her mother Cecelia Nolan was Canadian...Betty's grandfather, William H. Morris was born in Ticonderoga. His parents were French Canadian. Their names were Antoine Morris and Angeline Hubert Morris. They all were Catholics. Regards, Michael

French! I'm French. Names were beginning to show up on

my new family tree that were certainly new to me. Antoine and Angeline. There were none of those in my nurturing family. As time went on there were more names that had a different ring to them. Names like Jossette, Phoebe and Amelia.

3/2/2007

Hi Michael,

The (Betty's) obituary notice did not "attach" to your message, but that's okay. I went to the Public Library yesterday and was able to get it from the local newspaper's microfilm. It was a less than perfect image, but readable.

Thank you for the information on nationality. I am glad that the IRISH figure in the mix. The French-Canadian is a new twist, but interesting....

I have always known that I was adopted. How I knew the name is kind of vague. My adoption papers refer to me by the name MORRIS. When I was about 10 and deciding on a name to choose for Confirmation, I can remember my mother saying I might want to select ELIZABETH for my "mother" but I did not select that name. I took the name MARY instead. Strangely, I note that Mary was Betty's middle name. I have no idea how my mother knew her name, because it does not show up on any legal papers...

The obit notes Betty's daughter as being Mrs. Bruce Loucks – you mentioned her as being Arlene – do you know if she is still living here in Schenectady. There is an Arlene Loucks in the phone book, living at 1212 ZZZZZZ Avenue. I would not think of calling her unless she was open to the contact. If her mother had never related the stories of her past, it could be a devastating intrusion into her life...

Thank you for all the information you are sharing. You cannot know how much it means to me. Pat

It had only been five days since my first contact with Michael. Yet I had received so much information about my birth family. It seemed that with each e-mail I was coming to know this person. For years I had thought of Elizabeth as a sort of ghost from my past. Now she was a person who had family. And those family members had names. What I had never fantasized about was the possibility of having any sibling(s). My complete interest and curiosity had always focused on Elizabeth, my birth mother. Now I was aware that her daughter not only existed, but lived less than 15 minutes from my home. Caution still ruled my use of that information.

3/2/2007

Hi Pat,

... My mother wanted me to tell you that Betty had black hair and had olive complexion, also. She remembers your birth father was a very nice looking guy, but he refused to marry Betty. She thinks that was due to the fact that he wanted to be a professional boxer. She may come up with his name, yet. I think the last time my mother saw Betty was a few years before she died. Betty's hair was snow white.... Michael

3/2/2007

Good Morning, Michael,

Again, thank you and your mother for the information that you are streaming my way.

My hair color, as a younger person, was dark blond, nearly brown. Age, though, kind of levels the playing field and it is now white, and I keep it that way – can't be bothered with the coloring routine. Perhaps the blond hair color is a "gift" from the boxer boyfriend.

Although I have had NO knowledge of Betty until this week, she has been on my mind and in my prayers on a regular basis throughout the years, for as long as I can remember. Special times that I think about her are: on my birthday, on Mother's Day and on my adoption day. I have always recognized her as a special part of my life story. These remembrances will continue, but with a clearer image of the person, thanks to you. Pat

3/3/2007

Hi Pat,

...I am just as excited for you as you are for yourself. I am always happy when I find answers when I do the research on the family tree. It is sort of like Christmas happening all over again.

So Pat, you said you were a teacher. Is Walsh a married name and do you have children. Again f you don't want to answer these questions it is okay...

Michael

I could do no other than respond, with a brief sketch of who this stranger was that had suddenly been inserted into Michael's family story.

3/3/2007

Hi Michael,

... No, I don't mind answering questions about who I

AM since you are helping me to establish who I WAS. I never married (I guess you could call me an old maid – but don't) and have no children, but have had plenty of them in my life. I taught elementary school for over 30 years. For the last 16 years I have been the director of the Faith Formation program at my local Catholic Church. With great anticipation I am looking forward to retiring in 117 days (but who's counting!)

Since I was raised as an only child, I have no nieces or nephews – but lots of cousins with whom I keep in very close contact. I enjoy watching their children and grandchildren as they grow up. They are very much a part of my life. Having been adopted has not affected my place in the family. In fact, a cousin and I are sort of the family "historians" and have put together a pretty extensive and complete family tree, keeping it up to date as new arrivals are added. We spend a lot of time during the summer traipsing through old cemeteries and visiting the State Library of Genealogy in Albany. At this point there are 10 other adoptees in the next two generations of the family.

You have gathered quite a bit of information about me over this last week, but I know nothing of you. Could you tell me something of yourself? If you'd rather not, it is sufficient to know that you are a fellow genealogy enthusiast and that you are willing to share as much of that as intersects my life. That puts you pretty high on my scale of good people. Thanks, Pat

Michael responded with a verbal portrait of his family. He is the third of his parent's four sons. Michael mentioned that he was born in Glens Falls, NY on his Aunt Rose's 50th birthday. His three brothers, Bill, Peter and Andy are married and live in upstate New York and New England. Michael has lived in Florida for over 20 years and is not married. In his message he also gave me a brief sketch of each of his brother's families, their employment and their children. I was beginning to feel as if I knew these people, though they were still only names on paper. Even so, they were my second cousins. As I have said, cousins were very important to me.

3/4/2007

Hi Michael,

Well that was a pretty good sketch of you and your family. Thanks.

It was interesting to see that you were born on your Aunt Rose's birthday. By some strange coincidence, I was born on my adoptive mother's 39th birthday. She used to say, jokingly, that with 365 days in the year, why did I pick her birthday!?!?!? We shared that day for 50 years. My 51st birthday was strange, without sharing the day for the first time.

In trying to piece the parallel lines of genealogy together, I now see where your line joins the line that I fit into. This is all so interesting and fascinating. It has also become an all-consuming activity; putting it all in the computer and keeping a running record of the correspondence that has brought all these facts to light. I'm still bowled over by the fact that the story is unfolding and the pieces of the puzzle are falling into place, thanks to you. Pat

In his next letter, Michael gave me a complete listing of my (our) ancestry from Betty's great-great-grandparents forward through the descending five generations. Now I was beginning to see the family tree taking shape and spreading its roots and branches. Each name, dates of births, deaths and marriages were recorded in the data base on my computer. And entering my name as the child of Elizabeth Morris, I not only had a place in the ancestral line, but I now had six generations of history. This was a gift I had never expected to receive when I sent off that e-mail, barely a week before.

The correspondence between Michael and I continued on a daily basis. One of my points of curiosity was, of course, medical history. Michael's letters told of deaths from old age, heart condition, flu epidemic and accident. That seemed like a wide variety of causes of death and I was especially pleased to note that several of my biological ancestors had lived into their 90's and even to be over 100 years of age. There didn't appear to be any dominant cause of death, though there were several that noted some heart involvement.

I must interject here a humorous note that we came across in doing genealogical research on my nurturing family. An elderly aunt, it was noted in her obituary, had died at the age of 95, of "the cessation of her heart's pulsation." Now couldn't that be said ultimately of all end of life events!

3/6/2007

Good Morning, Michael,

Like I said before, I have gotten used to not being able to be specific about a family medical history, so continuing to not know is not a problem....Thanks for the information that you had. It doesn't seem that there is a strong tendency toward any medical problem. I can live with that (for a long time). Pat

That same day, Michael forwarded to me a picture of my great-grandparents. It had been taken around 1927 It showed a dear, elderly couple, standing in the yard of their home. I use the word elderly with caution, though. The years took their toll in those days, more than they seem to now. Great-grandmother Morris died at the age of 77, shortly after the tragic death of her son, in 1929. So in this picture she would have been about 75, which does not seem old, by today's standards.

The following day Michael was nice enough to send me a picture of his family. Though the picture had been taken ten years earlier, it put a face to the names I had recently come to know as members of my family. The people in the picture were my cousins. As I have said before and will repeat again, cousins have always been a significant part of my life. That continued to be the case as a new cousin introduced me to my new family.

3/9/2007

Hi Pat,

I'm glad you enjoyed seeing the pictures I sent. ... I will send more info about the Morris family. My mother said she often wondered what ever happened to the baby that Betty gave up. She is just as thrilled about you finding us as you are. No pressure, but I was wondering, in July when I come North, if you'd like to meet my mother and myself. Again, no pressure, it will be totally up to you. Michael

3/9/2007

Hi Michael,

Luckily, in our Genealogy quest, most of my cousins are interested...

Oh, Michael, I would love to meet your dear mother,

and you, of course. I cannot explain the range of emotions that envelop me, just knowing that there is someone who actually knew my "birth mother." July is pretty clear on my calendar, because I will be retiring on July 1. When I know when you are going to be up here, I will be sure to keep the time clear for whatever day suits you folks best. There is no rush on setting a day/time. I will MAKE it fit. I have waited 68 years for this and it is a high priority for me. Pat

To even the playing field, I sent Michael a picture of myself. It was a formal portrait, taken four years earlier, but it was still a valid representation of what I looked like.

3/9/2007

Hi Pat,

I got your picture. I am sending it to my brother to see if he is able to print it out and show it to my mother.

I plan on being up North between July 14 and 27. I know my mother would like to meet and talk to you, also... Looking forward to meeting you in July. Michael

3/10/2007

Good Morning, Michael,

It may be hard to find a family resemblance between myself and Betty since she did not live to be the age I am. Although your mother said she (Betty) had white hair the last time she saw her. Maybe some features will bear a hint of connectedness...I really appreciate your family's openness to the possibility of meeting. Pat

By this time, Michael had his whole family involved – his Mother, his sister-in-law, his brother, and one of his nephews. It was such an incredible feeling to realize that the extended McCall family was entering into this project as enthusiastically as Michael and I.

3/10/2007

Hi Pat,

I just wanted you to know that my sister-in-law printed out your picture and my nephew brought it to my mother. My mother said she saw Betty in you. She said your face was shaped like Betty's and other facial features are similar to Betty's.

Michael

3/12/2007

Good Morning, Michael,

Technology is surely amazing. The role it has played in my life in the past two weeks is unbelievable. That picture going from me to you, from you to your sister-in-law via Internet, then a hard copy to your mother (thanks to your nephew) and her response retracing the steps via phone and e-mail back to me in a little over 30 hours. It boggles the mind! I hope it didn't scare her!

I really appreciate all that your family is doing to make these things happen. I am so indebted to your mother for her clarity of memory and willingness to share those memories. So many people would just say, "We don't talk about those things," and close the door to all possibility of putting the pieces of the puzzle in place. The first couple of days of our correspondence I feared waking up and finding it had been a dream. But now I realize that it is real, and I am very glad that it is. Thanks to you. Pat

As it has been mentioned before and will come up again as this story unfolds, I cannot help thinking about my birth family when my birthday rolls around each year. In 2007 I was approaching this day with an entirely new perspective as I told Michael in an e-mail sent on my 68th birthday.

3/16/2007

Hi, Michael,

Today is one of those days when I think a lot about the circumstances of my coming into this big, wonderful world. As I said before, for many years, my birthday had been a time when I thought of and prayed for the person who gave me life. I had always imagined the circumstances to be that of a young, teen-aged girl, frightened and unprepared to face the responsibilities of motherhood without the structure of a family, yet courageous enough to give birth and release the child to a family to be loved and cared for. As the story has unfolded over the past couple of weeks, I realize that my "image" was a little off the mark. But I am still grateful to Betty for what she did on my behalf. And today, as I reflect on her life, she is no longer a phantom image, but a person who has a family history and people who have not forgotten her. You have truly made this a very happy birthday for me.

Funny, the common threads that are found where you least expect them. You mentioned that your Aunt Rose had a son who became a priest and later left the

*priesthood. I of course, was not a priest, but for over thirty years I was a Sister of St. Joseph. During that time I even taught at St. Mary's School in Glens Falls (1966-1967). I left the convent life in 1990, shortly after my mother died. I have no regrets about entering the convent, staying 30+ years or leaving. Everything happens for a reason, and I am happy with my choices.
... Pat*

From the information that Michael had shared, I learned that I was born ten days before Betty's 19th birthday. So she was not at the young teen ager as I had thought she might have been.

3/16/2007

Hi Pat,

I take it today's your birthday. A very, very, happy birthday to you. Well I'm very glad you are getting some answers to questions you've had over the past several years. I admire how you didn't want to search for your birth family while your parents were living. ... Yes, Betty gave you life but I can tell you had a GREAT WONDERFUL LIFE with your very loving parents.

*A VERY HAPPY BIRTHDAY TO YOU !!!! From a new found cousin and a very warm welcome to our family.
... Michael*

On March 26th Michael sent me a copy of his data-entries from the Family Tree Maker files. Now the information was coming through in an ordered manner and I was able to compare and complete the entries I had made from Michaels's previous e-mails. I thanked him for the information and made note of the fact that this was, indeed, Betty's birthday. She would have been 87 on that day.

Our correspondences continued on a nearly daily basis. Many times the news was of the weather, as we moved from Winter into Spring and Summer drew near. Michael told many anecdotal stories of the ancestors. Some stories bore more credibility than others. Some were family legends passed from generation without a firm basis. All were interesting. Each tale carried with it a clearer image of the family that I never knew, but to which I had a solid connection.

5/19/2007, Michael,

... I have begun to tell cousins (two of them) of my pursuit of my "other history." They share my joy and excitement of the findings that have unfolded, thanks to you. ... Pat

By late May, Michael and I exchanged our home addresses, phone and cell phone numbers. It seemed that every e-mail carried a reference to our upcoming meeting in July. It was evident that all involved were looking forward to that meeting.

6/10/ 2007

Hello Everyone (Michael wrote to all on his mailing list),

This morning my mother was taken to Glens Falls Hospital ER ... taken to Albany Medical Center for testing that could not be done in Glens Falls. A spinal tap showed bleeding in the brain.... Michael

6/10/2007

Oh Michael, I am so sorry to hear the news of your

Mother's illness. Know that she and your whole family will be in my prayers. The fact that medical attention was given to her so quickly will be in her favor. Albany Med is a top notch facility. She is in good hands. My heart aches for you, living so far away at a time when "closeness" is the thing you want and need the most. Although I do not know your Mother, she has played such an important part in my life these past four months that I will be forever grateful to her. On a positive note, I will continue to look forward to meeting her next month. Medical professionals and prayer are a pretty powerful combination. Keep me posted on her condition. Pat

6/12/2007

Hi,

My mother was released from the hospital this afternoon. The Doctors at Albany Med said there was no sign of stroke or bleeding in the brain. .... Michael

6/13/2007

Good Morning Michael,

What wonderful news, following a pretty scary couple of days. The move from GF Hospital to Albany Med was surely the best move. I'll bet your mother is VERY glad to be home. And you must feel much more at ease at your distant vantage point.

It won't be long now, until you will be up here to see your mother in person. And that will be very important to you and to her.

Thanks for the update. Good news is always welcome.

Pat

For the next several days our communications involved the challenge of contacting churches and cemeteries for their records. Working from a distance, Michael was finding that the keepers of the records did not fully grasp the importance of his quest. Although he had been doing genealogy work for a few years, wanting to share as much information as possible gave him an additional incentive.

6/14/2007

Hi Pat,

... I will be flying North on Saturday, July 14th and will return on Saturday, July 28th, which means we will have to make plans soon to meet....

Michael

6/14/2007

Hi Michael,

... In the period of time that you will be up North, the only commitment I have is for the weekend of July 20, 21, 22. Other than that, I have kept the calendar clear. Let me know what works for you folks. ***I will be there when and where you say ....***

Pat

Although Michael was sending me information daily, my cousin Ray and I continued to search local records and find out as much as we could about the family we now knew had moved to the Schenectady area. After each "find," I would send Michael the news we had unearthed.

6/15/2007

Hi Michael,

... Today while Ray and I were doing our GENEALOGY thing, we went to the library and looked up (in City Directories) where Betty had lived while in Schenectady. We came up with four different addresses. Then we went to see where these places were. Her husband, Walter was a bus driver for the Schenectady Transit Co. ...

Pat

And again,

6/22/2007

Michael,

I just returned from an exciting day in Hudson Falls /

Fort Edward area.

At the library I looked through several years of HF High School yearbooks (1934-1938) with no success. In most of the pictures of groups, the individuals in the pictures are not identified – teams, choirs, bands and class groupings.

We were able to trace (with City Directories) the Morris family's movements from place to place from 1923 through 1954, as well as their places of

47

employment.

At Union Cemetery we visited the graves of Betty and Walter (of course), Betty's parents and grandparents. It was a profitable day. But I didn't get much info that you didn't already have...

Pat

As June passed and July moved in, we were growing closer and closer to the day that I would meet Michael and his mother, Sarah. Each message we exchanged made reference to the rapidly approaching meeting. We both seemed to be looking forward to it with excited anticipation. Finally, the date was set. On July 19, 2007 I would meet members of my birth-family for the first time.

July 19, 2007, I traveled to Glens Falls where I would meet Michael and his mother, Sarah. It was a day I had looked forward to since first making contact with Michael five months earlier. And as the moment drew closer so many thoughts were rushing through my head. Since I was running a little early, I decided to stop at a nearby shopping mall to "waste time," to collect my thoughts and calm my nerves. The following journal notation was written at that time.

>10:36 AM – July 19, 2007.

>A gentle rain is falling and I am literally minutes from meeting for the first time, members of the MORRIS family. The people I will meet are a first cousin of my Birth Mother and her son.

>The odyssey that has brought me to this moment is still a blur of events and emotions which I will sort out in the days ahead.

I have gratitude for Betty's decision to place me in the care of a loving family. I have deep gratitude to Michael and Sarah for being open to the idea of sharing my ancestry with me, piecing my life together and answering many question that are as old as I am.

God, be with me as I make the short journey to this meeting. Your loving and protective hand has been with me and has brought me to this moment.

What a wonderful meeting it was. We were all completely at ease with each other and with the situation that had brought us together. Sarah shared stories of her youth and the things that she and Betty had done as children. We all went out to lunch and continued to unfold the stories of our lives. This was the first time I had met someone who had known my mother, and had such treasured memories of their times together. Before we parted ways, Michael gave me a picture of my birth-mother. She was standing on the front porch of her grandparents' home, a young woman of about 18. The picture was probably taken the year before I was born. In that picture, I saw my Mother's face for the first time. There are no words in the English language that can adequately describe the feelings that it stirred in me. Joy, excitement, peace, love, and gratitude lightly skirt the emotion, but do not grasp fully what my heart felt at that moment.

Upon leaving, I stopped at the mall parking lot again to let some of the emotion spill out. Some of it was noted as follows.

    1:45 PM Rain continues ~

    "You look just like your mother." I've never heard that before. And now I have a picture of Betty. We had a wonderful visit and I have come to put a "person" with the name ~ birth mother ~ Betty ~ Elizabeth, as I have called her for as long as I can remember

Once home and with time to reflect further on the visit with Michael and his mother, I put my thoughts into words in an e-mail to Mike the next day.

7/20/2007

Hi Michael,

I am still reeling from the experience of yesterday.

It was so good to finally meet you and your dear Mother.

There are just no words to express what I have felt over these past five months as the story of my life has unfolded. To finally have a picture of the woman who gave me life is a GIFT that I never dreamed would be possible. It has been such a blessing to unravel the mystery of who Betty was; who were the people who surrounded her as a child and as a young woman; where she lived and worked. She is no longer just a name on my adoption papers. BETTY MORRIS is a real person. Thanks to you, I have a new understanding of who that person was.

I have scanned and enlarged the picture you gave me. It will get a frame today and be placed on my dining room buffet with other family photos. The original is mounted in the front cover of my album of our correspondence and other findings of the research we have been

doing.

Again, Thank You for yesterday – the visit, the lunch, the picture – for everything.

Pat

Lest there be any misunderstanding, her name does not appear on my adoption papers. The reference is to the family name, Morris.

7/20/2007

Good Morning, Pat,

It was really great meeting you also. My Mother felt the same since she often wondered about you over the years. My mother said when you were walking to your car, you were tall like your birth father. She said Betty was a little taller than she was. Now I wished I had found the other picture of my mother and Betty so I could see the height difference.

... Well I will be keeping in touch with you and please feel free to call my mother or visit her. I know she will like that. I'm glad I found at least one photo of your mother.

Michael

Taking the information that Michael had so generously shared with me, I enlisted the companionship of my cousin, Ray Flanigan, to enlarge the information base that I had.

From city directories, obituary notices, marriage announcements and high school yearbooks, we traced the movements of the family around the upstate area of New York and then to city of Schenectady. City Directories gave us the various addresses where the young Richter family had lived. We made our way around the city taking pictures of these homes and tried to piece together the pattern of their lives, both in the Glens Falls area and after their move to Schenectady. We were able to identify the employment patterns as well. City Directories soon gave way to phone books and were no longer printed annually. The local library did not stock the yearly phone book collection. I now had a fairly good idea of who these people were. But they still remained only names on paper.

The e-mail correspondence with Michael continued as I made new discoveries. He in turn, supplied me with additional facts and anecdotal information. With each new piece of information, I gained further insight into the family from which I had come. Although I had only met Michael and his mother Sarah, the people on the family tree were becoming real to me.

As new names and relationships were revealed through Michael's kindness, I wanted to know all I could glean from various sources about these people. Betty's mother, Ida, had lived with Betty and her family in Schenectady. From Michael I learned that Ida had died in Schenectady in 1958. So I began a search for her obituary in our local paper. I reported this to Michael.

7/27/2007

> *I went to the State Library today. I managed to get through January, February and March of 1958 newspapers without finding Ida's obit. It will be just as easy to go to the Schenectady Public Library and continue the search. With my luck, she died at the end of December!*
>
> *Pat*

8/1/2007

Good Morning, Michael,

> *Our searches on Thursday didn't yield any new information. I've made it through August 1958 in the Schenectady Gazette with no obit for Ida Morris. It is possible that they didn't run an obituary in Schenectady since she was from and returning to the North country. But they usually do carry the information locally when the death occurs here.*
>
> *We also looked through several years of yearbooks without finding any Arlene Richter....*
>
> *Pat*

Throughout my life, when thinking of the conditions of my birth, I never entertained the possibility of having siblings. I had always wanted to have a brother or sister, but was resigned to the fact that that would never happen. I had been born on my adoptive mother's 39th birthday. Enlarging the family with another infant through the process of adoption would be nearly impossible, considering her age. With the knowledge that I did, indeed, have a sibling, I was now faced with a longing that I had never experienced before. I HAD to find the child who was born to my mother in 1950. She had graduated from high school in 1968 and married in the Fall of that same year. She lived in the Bellevue section of Schenectady, mere blocks from where I had lived for 13 years, from 1978 through 1991.

By August of 2007, I was getting very anxious to know as much as I could about my birth mother. There was only one person that I knew of who could fill in the blanks and answer the questions that I had. It was at this point that I asked Michael to make a direct contact with my mother's daughter, Arlene.

8/12/2007 1:30 PM

Good Afternoon, Michael,

> *...Since you are doing family research, is there any chance that you would contact her (Arlene) for information to complete your records? Such items as the death date of her Grandmother Ida? Her children's names? Any items of interest she might be willing to share about her mother?*
>
> *I realize you have not been in contact with that extension of the family, but with all the interest in Family Trees & Heritage, she might be open to the inquiry. No pressure – just a selfish thought.*

Pat

8/12/2007 6:33 PM

Hi, Pat,

> *I haven't really thought about contacting Arlene, but I guess it would be worth a try. There is nothing to lose. We have a fifty-fifty chance that she may be of some help. I have written a rough draft of a letter to send her. I will attach it to this e-mail to see what you think of it. Please, make any changes if you like. Please let me know what you think of the letter and if you have any suggestions. ...*

Michael

8/12/2007 7:00 PM

Hi Michael,

That was a great letter.

In true school teacher style, I made a couple of corrections/suggestions. ...

Thanks for agreeing to seek information from her. It will be interesting to see if she is interested and cooperative. And if so, what you can find out. As you said, "We've got nothing to lose." Pat

The following is the text of the letter which Michael sent to Arlene. It is being inserted here in the event that someone who is traveling this road to discovery needs some idea of how to ask for information. It is not intended to be a model for the use of others, but simply a suggestion of an approach that might result in gaining some useful information.

August 2007

Dear Arlene,

Please let me introduce myself. My name is Michael McCall and we happen to be second cousins. My grandmother Celia Morris VanVranken and your grandfather, William Morris were sister and brother. My mother, Sarah VanVranken and your mother Betty Morris Richter were first cousins and grew up more or less in the same neighborhood. Betty and your Uncle Vincent, as children, often visited my mother's family in Hudson Falls, NY.

The reason I'm writing you, I've been working on a Family Tree project for close to four years. I now realize I really need to contact cousins to ask for their help and input if they so desire. Since I have been doing this research I have realized that public records and Ancestry.com can help so much with family members that lived years back, but they're not much of any help with present day family members. My mother is the last of the first cousins on the Morris side of the family and I have more or less exhausted her memory (she is 87). What I'm looking for are names, dates and places of birth, death and marriages. The way I discovered you was that my mother knew Betty and Walter had a daughter that lived in Schenectady. She wasn't sure of your name which I ended up finding in your mother's obituary.

I'm willing to send to you what I have so far with the Morris side of the family. I'm sure you know they are basically French-Canadian and Irish. If you have computer access, I would be able to send this info via e-mail. Our great-great-grandparents Morris were from St. Catherine in Canada and finally settled in Fort Edward, NY.

They ran a boarding house and their son, our great-grandfather, William Morris, worked on the barge canals between NY State and Canada. Our great-grandmother Mary McClosky Morris's father, John, was born and raised in Ireland and he settled in Argyle, NY. He was also a veteran of the Civil War.

I usually find a date of death and request the obituary for that person. I'm having problems locating one for your Grandmother, Ida. My mother thinks she moved to Schenectady and lived with your parents at the time of her death in 1958. However the Union Cemetery and the Town Clerk's office in Ft. Edward have no records as to where or when she died nor do the local funeral homes in Hudson Falls. I know it was in 1958 due to the fact that I know where the grave site is. I do not know how old you were at the time of her death, but was hoping for a least a month in 1958 that she died and the location where she was living at the time. If you have any anecdotal memories of your parents or grandmother, they could be added to the family records.

I do hope you are interested in the family history and will be able to help me with this research. I will give you ways you may contact me if you wish to.

Name   Phone Number

Address   E-Mail address

I will appreciate any help you are able to give to me and hope to hear from you soon.

While awaiting a response from Arlene to Michael, I continued my search for any information I could find. Much of my research was futile and at other times I hit paydirt. Each new nugget of information was passed on to Michael as well as the brick-wall experiences.

8/15/2007

Hi, Michael,

... I have completed looking through the 1958

Schenectady newspapers for an obit for Ida R. Morris, with no success

They probably only ran it in Glens Falls papers since that was her native area. Oh well, it was worth the try.

In an attempt to find Arlene in a High School yearbook, we hit another brick wall. Since she was born in 1950, it is most likely that she would have graduated from high school in 1967 or 1968. Strangely enough, those are the 2 years missing from the Library's yearbook collection. ...

Pat

Due to the fact that Michael was in the process of moving to a new home, he did not mail the letter to Arlene until late August. It was not long before I received a phone call from Michael informing me that he had gotten a response from her.

9/5/2007

Hi, Michael,

Your call the other day with news of Arlene's response has given me cause for excitement. ... I hope that she will share with you some information about her (our) mother. Maybe even a picture of her, later in life. I am especially interested in and concerned about the cause of her early death. The primary motivation behind my looking for my birth ancestry was for the medical history that would be directly in my blood line. The phrase "died unexpectedly" in her obit, leaves a lot of questions unanswered and the possibilities limitless. If she does come through with anything, I would really appreciate hearing of it.

I can only say that the way the story has unfolded over the past seven months far exceeds anything I could ever have hoped for or expected, thanks to you. —Pat

9/5/2007

Hi, Pat,

I sent Arlene copies of the genealogy report. Response was very short and sweet. She said she could tell I had put a lot of work into it and had printed copies so she could wrap her mind around everything and she hoped we would keep in touch. I did a little prodding by sending her a picture of my family so she could put a face with the name, thinking she would do the same on her end, but her response was, "What a nice looking group." I think I will hold off for a few days before contacting her again, hoping she will get in touch with me with questions or more info first. ... Well, if we have to sit tight for a little longer that is okay, too. I may start asking her for info on her Uncle Vincent's daughter's family when I do get in touch with her again, before getting into the real nitty-gritty.

Michael

9/5/2007

Hi, Again, Michael,

I fully subscribe to your perceptions about proceeding with your contact with Arlene. She has accepted the contact. While I'm glad she responded, I can understand her being cautious in her correspondence. Even though you are cousins, you are virtual strangers. It will all come together – eventually.

Good Night,

Pat

9/18/2007

Hi, Pat,

I just sent Arlene another dose of Family History. I did her grandfather's side of the family. I'm hoping that she will start giving me a few bits of info on her mother. I haven't asked any personal questions other than if she is in contact with her Uncle Vincent's daughter. I put in some causes of death in the history to see if she volunteers any info on her mother's death. ...

Michael

During this time of knowing of Arlene, but before we had made any kind of contact, I had driven by her home several times. What struck me immediately was the fact that her house bears an uncanny likeness to mine. Both are small bungalow style houses with enclosed front porches. Both are located on quiet side streets off main roads. In telling the story to others, jokingly, the word *stalking* has come up. It must be admitted, that I was hoping to catch a glimpse of this person who may have been my sister.

9/18/2007

Hi, Michael,

Slow and easy does it! It will be nice if she establishes a correspondence with you that yields some information. But I think you are right in expecting to get more answers by NOT asking the questions.

This afternoon I was in Arlene's part of town running errands – drove past her house. What is really uncanny is that her house is almost exactly like mine. It is the same size and style and both are vinyl sided with enclosed porches. Don't panic . . . I'm not going to do anything foolish. ... Pat

During another research session at the Schenectady County Library I was looking through the microfilms of the Schenectady Gazette for the Fall of 1968. Michael had indicated that Arlene had married shortly after her graduation from Mont Pleasant High School. Using the microfilm reader is a tedious task, especially with bifocals. Nevertheless, I sped past the daily news of each edition and found the society pages. Surely they would announce the marriage in the paper.

I continued to make frequent trips to the library, scanning the microfilm files of the Schenectady Gazette for any clue or information I could glean on this person I would eventually know as my sister, but who was still a virtual phantom character in my search.

My perseverance did not go unrewarded. There it was. A picture of the bride was accompanied by a descriptive article which told of the bride's gown and those of her attendants, the groomsmen, the reception and their planned wedding trip to northern New York. But all that was insignificant at the moment. All I could see, all I could focus on was the headline. It read: Arlene Patricia Richter Bride of Bruce A. Loucks. I let out an audible gasp. Ray came from a nearby reader to see what I had found. There it was, in black and white. Arlene's middle name was Patricia. Whatever the reason for her carrying that name, my name, it was a truly high point of my search. It was the first real glimpse I had of this mystery sister and into her life.

Then I would send this message to Michael.

9/27/2007

Hi, Michael,

Just a quick note with some updated information.

Arlene PATRICIA Richter married Bruce A. Loucks at Saint Paul's Episcopal Church in Schenectady on September 8, 1968.

The newspaper image was of pretty poor quality and the printer at the library was having a bad day. I will try to send you the image and the text of the article this evening.

Her middle name took my attention. **Patricia** *must have been an important name in Betty's life if she used it for two of her children. It would be interesting to know that story! Middle names don't show up too often in society page articles, but there it is!*

Pat

Later that evening, after re-scanning the picture and article, I sent Michael the notice, as it had appeared in the paper 39 years earlier. It did not escape my notice that I had found the article announcing Arlene's wedding on September 27, 2007, noting that it had appeared in the paper on September 27, 1968.

In our continued correspondence, Michael and I explored the question of Arlene's middle name.

> *9/27/2007*
>
> *Hi Pat,*
>
> *So Betty named you when you were born. I didn't really know how that worked; if a mother names a child or if the adoptive parents named the baby.*
>
> *So Betty, I feel, did think of you over the years, especially since she gave Arlene the middle name of Patricia. ...*
>
> *Michael*

> *9/27/2007*
>
> *Hi, Again,*
>
> *Yes, I came already named. As I understand it, my parents had the option of changing my name, but since I was born the day before St. Patrick's and they were quite attached to their Irish heritage, they were satisfied with their little Patricia. My legal papers identify me as Patricia Ann Morris. ...*
>
> *Pat*

Our e-mails continued from day to day and week to week. There were days when three or four messages would go back and forth between us. Then there might be a period of a few days when there was no news coming in and no news for me to share. Those days seemed to be the longest days. I was anxious to hear anything that might bring me more and more into the reality of having and knowing about my family of origin.

In July of 2007 I sent to the State of New York State Department of Health requesting the Death Certificate of Elizabeth Mary Morris. Although I am not one to make frequent visits to the graves of deceased family members, on October 19, 2007, I decided to travel to Hudson Falls, to visit the grave of my birth mother. This was the 30th anniversary of her death and I felt the need to spend some time in quiet reflection at her grave. It was an emotional visit. Standing there, I had a long conversation with the woman I had known only for the decision she had made, nearly 70 years before. She had been in the difficult position of being pregnant, single and not able, at that time, to care for a child. She courageously relinquished her parental rights, to place this child in the care of the Sisters of Saint Joseph at St. Joseph's Infant Home in Troy, NY, with the belief that they would find a good home for her child. There was so much I wanted her to know. I had had a loving family. I had had many interesting life experiences and I was happy with my life, in general. A mother needs to know these things about her child.

Upon arriving home that day, I found in the mail box, a copy of the death certificate I had requested three months earlier. This document offered the first glimpse into a familial medical history. Based upon the information on the death certificate, I learned that Elizabeth had died of "cardiac arrest consistent with coronary artery heart disease." Armed with this knowledge, I notified my own primary care physician of the medical background. She then arranged for an appointment with a cardiologist to establish baseline readings and rule out any heart condition at that time. Anyone who has ever visited a doctor's office is familiar with the intake questionnaire. It seems it is filled out annually, even though basic information has not changed within the last year. My birth date did not change. Childhood diseases and prior surgeries, allergies and health habits do not change. But now I could say that I had a significant medical history.

I had known people with family history of cancer who were convinced that they would die of cancer. I can remember joking that one person in particular was so sure of death by cancer, that if she died of another cause, she'd come back for a "do over." Since I had no idea of what claimed the life of any blood-family member, I did not anxiously await the onset of any dreaded disease. In reality, though, as I aged and matured I wanted to know what precautions I should take to offset whatever predisposition I might have.

Upon arriving home from my trip to Union Cemetery, I sent Michael this report.

10/19/2007

Hi, Michael,

Today is the 30th anniversary of Betty's death. I decided that it would be a good time for me to visit the cemetery, bring some flowers and spend some time "visiting" with her. I am not one to visit cemeteries on a regular basis (other than our genealogy treks), but I felt the need to spend some time with Betty and to sort of talk things over with her. Call me crazy if you want. It was an unseasonably hot and humid day with a threat of severe storms, so I headed back home when I was *ready. Originally I thought I would call your Mother and see if she would be up to a visitor. But I got a later start than I had planned on, and with the weather situation as it was, I thought it wiser to not delay my homeward trip.*

When I got home, I had, in the mail, a copy of Betty's death certificate. I had requested it several months ago and had pretty much abandoned any hope of getting it. They are not supposed to be issued to genealogical requests until after 50 years. In any case, I got the certificate and the information I was seeking: cause of death – cardiac arrest resulting from artery heart disease determined by autopsy. It is the info I was looking for but not the information that I wanted!

Pat

In carefully reviewing each message from Michael, I noted that in the branches of the family tree there was a wide range of years lived. For example, there was a pair of sisters, Ruth and Helen, who lived to be 100 and 95 respectively. The records from Michael, as well as cemetery markers revealed the deaths of others who lived a very short life. Accidents accounted for some of the deaths early in life. Our grandfather was killed in a railroad accident at a lumber mill in Maine. I decided to focus on those with longevity and claim that as my heritage.

In my continued research, I was able to locate Arlene's high school yearbook. It showed a lovely young lady. But as much as I strained to find it, I saw no family resemblance to me. Taking my own high school picture for comparison did not help. Perhaps because I had never had someone with features that resembled mine, I didn't know how to look for them.

As with each of my findings, I sent an e-mail to Michael that evening to inform him of the news.

> *11/5/2007*
>
> *Hi Michael,*
>
> *I went to the Library today and looked in the 1968 yearbook for Arlene's picture. Unfortunately the copier was still not working, so I took this with my cell phone camera – hence the lack of clarity. Maybe someday I'll go back and try to copy it, then scan it when I get home, for a better image.*
>
> *She is really quite an attractive young lady. But even with a picture, I don't think I'd know her if I passed her on the street. Nearly 40 years has probably changed her, at least a little.*
>
> *Take care,*
>
> *Pat*

During the Christmas holiday season I did a lot of thinking about the situation in which I now found myself. I knew that I had a half-sister. I knew that she also carried my name, though assigned to a middle name. I knew where she lived. There was still a very important question to which we did not have the answer. Was Arlene ever told, by her Mother, that she had had a child earlier in her life?

As with so many of my thoughts, I sent it off to Michael for his slant.

> *1/3/2008*
>
> *Hi, Michael,*
>
> *... I had hoped that Arlene might have been a little*

more informative about her family by now. Of course, she doesn't know that we are (I'm) waiting for an indication that she might be aware of her mother's other child.

I have been struggling with the idea of writing to her with this question: "I have been doing family research and have reason to believe that your mother might be my birth mother. Do you have reason to believe that this is not possible or that, in fact, it could be? I would like to hear from you in either case."

Due to the fact that Arlene's middle name is Patricia, I have a feeling that Betty may have explained the reason for that choice – or not. By saying that she does NOT believe that it is the case, I would accept the decision that Betty took her secret to the grave. But if there is a chance that she had spoken of her earlier history, she may have wished to know what became of that first child and may have passed the task of answering the question on to Arlene.

I have not acted on this urge, and would not make any reference to having gotten any information from you via Ancestry.com. What are your thoughts on this?

Pat

Unfortunately, Michael's response to this message has been lost. In a nearly two year correspondence, it appears to be the only one to have escaped being copied and preserved. The essence of his response was to advise me against making any kind of contact with Arlene. His expressed fear was that it could jeopardize their newly formed relationship. Michael suggested that I work through the State Adoption Registry, if that is available in New York.

> *1/4/2008*
>
> *Good Morning, Michael,*
>
> *Thank you for our clear-headed and reasonable caution regarding contacting Arlene. I will follow your advice and put the matter on the back burner indefinitely. There is no point in setting a future date to anticipate.*
>
> *There is an Adoption Registry in NY State. It carries a $75 fee (perhaps more by now-that was ten years ago), for any contact information. Non-identifying info is free, but I always doubted that information, such as medical records, would have been filed. I'm not sure whether this service was available 30 years ago, to give Betty a chance to register with the Registry, even if she wanted. I will consider doing the necessary paper-work for that process. In the past, I have always stopped short of actually filing it because I figured there would not be a search in process from the birth family. You are right, it would be best to go that route first. ...*
> *Pat*

Michael related the story of a friend who was reunited with his birth sibling, but no real relationship was established. The dream of a reunion was dashed. Although there were a couple of meetings with the birth-mother, they did not bond on any level.

My own experience was as an observer of another reunion

gone terribly bad.

1/5/2008

Good Morning, Michael,

"Reunions" are very fragile events, I realize. Caution is the best route to take.

I knew a young woman who worked for the State, accessed her sealed records and contacted her birth mother, with tragic results. The elder woman made it clear that she had done what she felt was best at the time, later married, raised a family, and had not shared the information with her family. She said she would get a restraining order against her "daughter" if she made contact again. Of course, the process was done in an underhanded and illegal way, but the devastation was unbelievable for the daughter. She saw it as a second rejection by the woman who, she thought, should have an unconditional love for her. When in fact, the unconditional love was shown when she gave her to a family who could provide a safe, loving home when she, herself, could not.

I have submitted the papers to the NY State Adoption Registry. It will only yield information IF either Betty or Arlene have also registered with the hope for, and permission to make, a connection. The papers clearly state that it may take as long as six months to process the information and there may never be an outcome. Well, I haven't known anything all these years, so I guess I can wait some more. There is also a category called non-identifying information which will be available immediately, if on file, and with the permission of

> *the adoption agency (Catholic Charities). That includes such things as religion, ethnicity, race, education, occupation, etc., of the birth parents.*
>
> *In the meantime, I have the information that you have been so willing to share. That gives me some idea of where I came from and has truly been one of the greatest processes of my life. Thanks. Pat*

It must be noted here that the access to adoption records can vary from state to state. In some states the records are available with certain restrictions. Some will release information ONLY to siblings who are searching for their siblings or half-siblings. The search may not be initiated by the birth parent. Other states will allow information shared between birth-parent and child released for adoption, once consent has been given by both parties. In some states, like New York, adoption records are "forever sealed." There have been changes made in some states that did not have "forever sealed" records. They may have specified the number of years to pass before a search can be initiated. States like Maine have since modified the waiting period. If you are looking to begin a search for a child or parent or siblings, check with the adoption laws in the state in which the adoption took place.

Many couples today are entering into open adoptions. This allows the birth parent(s) to know the adopting family. In many cases a lasting bond is formed between the adults, and regular visits take place. This also opens the door to securing further information as the child ages. Again, medical issues are more readily available as the birth-parent ages and encounters significant issues like cancer, heart disease, diabetes, or Alzheimer's disease. This knowledge is very important in anyone's life. Being unaware of major risk factors is an unfortunate outcome of sealed adoptions. Whether or not birth-parents are being counseled to keep their information current, for the benefit of the child, I am not sure. What I am sure of is that it would be the responsible thing to do.

Noting the fact that our correspondence had been on-going for a year, I wrote to Michael:

1/27/2008

Good Morning, Michael,

...This date marks the day, one year ago, when I first connected with you. It has been a wonderful year in my life. The information that I have gathered, thanks to you, is information that I never thought I would ever have. I hope that sometime in the not too distant future, that the door will open for me to contact Arlene and be able to learn more about Betty. Time will tell if that is meant to be. . . .
Take care,

Pat

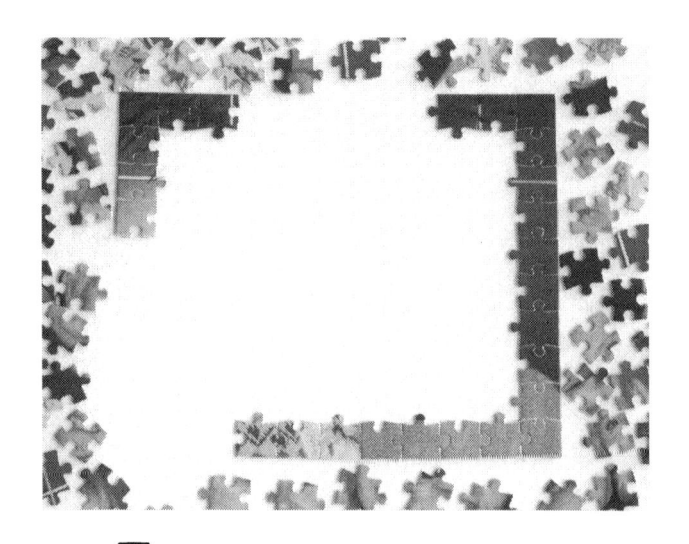

A My happy story begins in 2007. I received a letter of introduction from a man, Michael McCall, saying that he was the son of my mother's cousin, Sarah, and he was doing genealogy on the Morris family. Sarah had pretty much grown up with my mother and I remember my mother mentioning her from time to time, but I had never met her. She was now in an assisted-living facility in Glens Falls. Michael said he would send me all the information he had on the Morris's and he wanted to know if I had any additional information or stories about any of our relatives that could be included. Since I had never asked questions, I had nothing.

A point has to be made right here. ASK QUESTIONS! Find out about your family. Not that you'll hear information like this, but just to <u>know</u> about your family. I don't think my mother ever asked about her family history either. I had asked her one time about nationalities and she didn't know. She knew my father's parents were German and Dutch, but nothing about her own family. Since meeting Michael, I found out that my great-great-grandparents McCloskey came from Ireland and my great-great-grandparents Hubert from Canada. Who knew? Not me.

Michael had pages and pages of information on my mother's family. Not only did he have names, birth dates and birth places of relatives back five generations, but he also had stories about some of them, too. I was feeling a real "family" connection to these people, most of whom I had never met. Most of the relatives I knew were from my Grandmother Morris' side of the family (the Gray's) and Michael was detailing my Grandfather Morris' side. Since my grandfather was killed in 1929, when my mother was just 9 years old, my grandmother may have lost contact with Morris relatives over the years, except for those who lived nearby. I do have a notebook which my grandmother kept that listed all births, deaths and marriages on her side of the family. However, I had no additional information for Mike to include about the Morris's – he knew more than I did! Although I had no idea how MUCH more he knew than I did!

Thinking of it now, and rereading correspondence I received from Michael, it must have been frustrating for him (to say nothing of Pat) that I had no information to share. Each e-mail I received from him ended with some form of "if you have any questions…" or "if you have anything to add…" Even though I had no idea what he knew I felt badly, embarrassed, actually, that I lacked any general knowledge of my mother's family. I had no stories to share, other than my camping story, that is, and I wasn't sure it would be appropriate for me to share that one. Maybe later.

But we began a very nice relationship – here was a cousin I didn't know I had! We e-mailed each other very often and I looked forward to meeting him and his mother the following summer, when he would come up north from Florida to visit. I was very excited to meet Sarah; she was the last person I knew of who had known my mother "back in the day."

When the day finally came when I was to meet them for lunch, I was very excited. Nervous, too. These were relatives, and fairly CLOSE relatives, whom I had never even met. I was actually a bit uncomfortable during our meeting because of the fact that Michael had done so much work over so many years and I had nothing to add to our family history. I remember my mother speaking of Sarah over the years and I knew they had been quite close when they were young, so I was anxious to meet her. I have to say I was hoping that, when I saw her, I'd see some resemblance to my mother, which I did not. They were only cousins after all – I don't look like my cousins either. But we had a nice visit, with only a few instances of awkward silence on my part, and Sarah shared a couple stories of her time with my mother and we chatted about my aunt and uncle.

It's funny to think back and realize that they knew about my sister then, but couldn't say anything to me. It must have been a bit uncomfortable for them and explains some of those silences. If I had been in their place, I don't know if I could have done it at all. I might just have come up with excuses not to meet.

St. Joseph's Infant Home, South Troy

1893	Founded at Glenmore location – 5 Infants
July 1895	Children moved to new site
December 1895	Building destroyed by fire – all residents safely removed & returned to Glenmore
January 1898	New building occupied
1963	Infant Home Closed

December 30, 1939

The day I left St. Joseph's Infant Home and was brought to my new home at age 9 months

Scouting . . .

Pat in Girl Scout uniform 1951

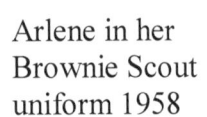

Arlene in her Brownie Scout uniform 1958

As Babies . . .

Our Mother, Betty

age 6 months

1920

Pat

Age 1 year

1940

Arlene

age 9 months

1950

Sisters . . .

Following our first Fourth of July trip to a cousin's home in Connecticut, this picture was sent as a memento of the visit. Taken from a fair distance away, our common, relaxed stance is evident.

Photo by Mary Helen Millham 07.04.2009

Betty . . .

July 19, 2007

The first time I saw the face of my Mother.

The picture was undated, but it was probably taken in 1938, the year before Pat was born.

Betty with her cousin, Sarah, at age 16.
1936

High School Senior Pictures

<   Pat – 1957

Saint Joseph's Academy

Schenectady, NY

Arlene - 1968 >

Mont Pleasant HS

Schenectady, NY

Good Times With Our Sister Mentors

After brunch at the Gideon Putnam in Saratoga Springs, NY

Maryanne, Arlene, Pat, Carolynn

A day trip on the Saratoga & North Creek RR.

Arlene, Maryanne, Conductor, Carolynn, Pat

At one of our early Craft Fairs – December 2010

Our First Booth at Artique Co-Op in Clifton Park, NY

P   My cousin, Raymond, had entered into the research with enthusiasm. But when I suggested that I would like to contact this mystery sister, he strongly advised against it, as did Michael. Each in his own way had suggested that it would be hurtful if I was "rejected" and the search would have a sad ending. Michael was also concerned that it might reflect unfavorably on him if Arlene felt he had been less than forthcoming in his seeking information from her. Both had my best interest at heart and so I held my desire in check, until . . .

In November of 2008 I mailed a letter to Arlene, expressing my belief that her mother may have been my birth mother.

In this letter, I had given Arlene every opportunity to "close the door," if she felt that I had contacted her in error. That was not what happened.

Patricia A. Walsh

XXXXX Street

City, State

November 8, 2008

Dear Arlene,

Please allow me to introduce myself. As you can see from the header, my name is Patricia Walsh – Pat, to my friends.

First, by way of explanation, I am 69 years old. As an infant, I was adopted by a wonderful man and woman. Since their deaths (in 1959 and 1990), I have been on a quest for information of my birth parents. That search has brought me to you for possible help with a solution.

I am writing to you in the hopes of finding the answer to a few questions. After years of researching the little information that I had, I have arrived at the possibility that your Mother, Elizabeth Morris Richter, may have been my birth mother. My request of you is: if you feel or know that this could be possible or if you feel strongly that it is not likely, nor possible, I would appreciate it if you would let me know.

I do not wish to interfere with or disrupt your family or any family. I have the utmost respect and gratitude to my birth mother and wish that I had had the opportunity to thank her for the choice she made on my behalf.

Again, I would like to hear from you, whether you think the possibility exists or if you feel that I have reached you in error.

I sincerely thank you,

Pat

E-Mail: XXXX123@XXX.com

Phone: 393-XXXX
Cell: 339-XXXX

In a note to myself in the journal of this journey, I wrote the following:

> 11/8/2008
>
> After much thought, mental arguments pro and con, and against the advice of Michael and Raymond, I mailed the letter to Arlene this afternoon.
>
> This has been a constant pre-occupation for me. I do not want to miss out on the chance that Arlene may have been told of her half-sister and perhaps, even given directives as to what she should do if that "stranger" came into her life. If she has no knowledge of her mother's previous child, I will let the subject drop and considered to be the secret buried with her (our) Mother.
>
> My sincere hope is that she will have heard of me and be curious enough to open the door to contact. I have so many questions about Betty – who she was; what she was like; what did she like to do; did she have hobbies; could I have a picture of her.
>
> This does not come without apprehension on my part. I am anxious to know the outcome of sending the letter and I am, somewhere deep inside, afraid that it might not end pleasantly. But it is worth the chance; the chance for a contact with the sister I never knew; the only person to whom I am actually, biologically connected.
>
> I have not told Michael of mailing the letter. Many months ago he advised against it, fearing that his newly established contact with Arlene might be jeopardized, if she realized that I got significant information from him. Now, ten months later, I feel that I can substantiate obtaining the connective

information via research I have done.

Que sera, sera! What will be, will be!

[Once I hear from Arlene, I will tell both Michael and Raymond of the outcome]

The mailing of this letter was not a random act. It was a carefully calculated time. November 8 was on a Saturday. The following Monday was the observed holiday of Veteran's day, and thus, there would be no mail delivery. Tuesday was my day off from work. That would be the day the letter would be delivered to Arlene. In my mind I reasoned that, if Arlene received the letter and wished to respond, I would be there to receive the phone call or e-mail. My hopes were high, but tempered with the realization that this might be a crashing end to my search.

It must be stated here that this next entry is outside my usual experience. Yet it is a strong part of our story and so I have been advised to include the narrative.

I had a very dear friend whose friendship had spanned forty years. I had told Sister Rose of my search and had kept her apprised of every new finding as it came along. She shared my excitement. Having worked at the Infant Home she was familiar with the process through which my parents had gone. She was also very much aware of my yearning to make contact with Arlene. She knew, too, of the counsel that I received from both Ray and Mike against that contact..

In mid-August of 2008, Sister Rose and I vacationed along the coast in New Hampshire and Maine. Our annual trip always included a stop at L.L. Bean in Freeport. Sightseeing, beach-combing and searching for coastal lighthouses filled our carefree days by the Atlantic Ocean. About three weeks after we returned from our vacation that year Sister Rose died suddenly. To say that I was shocked would be an understatement. I was devastated.

The following weeks were very difficult. I can honestly say that I hold Sister Rose directly responsible for my honoring the urge to send the letter I had written so many months before. I had no clear experience of Rose's intervention. But as I continued my correspondence with Michael, my longing to reach out to Arlene grew stronger and stronger. I like to imagine that she sought out my birth Mother and saw that it was time for me to make the connection and that she nudged me in that direction. It would be important for our Mother to know that her two daughters had met and were forming a bond. Seeing that I had lost a friend, Sister Rose saw to it that the void would be quickly filled with a sister who would become a new and treasured friend.

A In November, 2008, I received a letter that, once again, began with an introduction – how strange was that? This letter went on to say that, with the "little information" she had, she believed that my mother may have been her birth mother. I had to read that again. My mother may have been her birth mother. There are absolutely no words to explain how I felt at that moment. The only thing I can say is that I was stunned. I know I had a strange look on my face because my husband asked what was wrong. I handed him the letter and saw what must have been the same look come over his face. We just stared at each other. I don't know how many times I re-read that letter. We were both absolutely speechless! This happens on TV, not in real life. And certainly not to me! And her name was Patricia, which is my middle name. PLUS, she lived about 10 minutes away from me! Yes, I was skeptical, but never suspicious. Just from the way her letter was written, I knew she was truly searching for her birth mother, this was not a scam. She gave me ample opportunity to say I didn't think it was possible. But my parents weren't married until my mother was **28** and I wasn't born until she was 30. She had a whole *life* before I came along, so I couldn't just dismiss it. My husband and I agreed that I had to meet her and hear what she had to say. For me, there was never an option of not meeting her. Even if she had been mistaken, she deserved to know that. I had even decided that, if Pat wanted to, we could have a **DNA** test.

She needed answers.

PThat evening my e-mail server indicated that a new message had arrived. It bore the identification – Arlene Loucks. My heart skipped a beat. Maybe two or three beats. With unbearable excitement and trepidation, I opened the letter, unsure of what I would find.

I found a warm response. Arlene's message gave no indication that she may have known from her mother that a child had been born to her mother earlier in her life. But neither was there a flat-out rejection of the possibility. Instead, she simply asked, "If you don't mind, I'd really be interested in knowing what info you have that led you to my mother." To me, this was certainly a fair and reasonable request.

This started a volley of e-mails between Arlene and me. My immediate response gave her the data that I had compiled over the years. These facts, fragmented though they were, had given me the first glimmer of hope that I would be able to locate my birth family.

A The very next thing I did was e-mail Michael to ask if he thought his mother would know anything about this. I thought it was SO lucky that Michael had contacted me the previous year and that, at 88, Sarah was still sharp as a tack. I had absolutely no one else I could ask. Pat and I e-mailed each other many times the rest of that and subsequent afternoons and evenings and we eventually set up a day and time to meet at a local restaurant. It seems strange now, but I was actually hesitant to mention to Pat that I contacted a cousin in Florida. I didn't want her to think I didn't trust her. But keep in mind that I didn't know her, I hadn't even spoken to her on the phone. You hear so much about scams people try to perpetrate on unsuspecting individuals and, for all I knew, this person may not have even been a woman! What eased my mind a bit was that she had included her phone numbers, both home and cell, in her letter, although I was much too nervous to actually speak with her.

When I checked my e-mail the next morning, I had an answer from Michael. He said he had spoken with his mother and she said, yes, this was true. She remembered that my mother had a baby when she was 18 or 19; the father hadn't been ready to settle down with a wife and child – he had plans for his life, he had plans of becoming a boxer. Sarah remembered that my mother had gone away to a home for unwed mothers in Troy, NY, to have the baby and gave it up for adoption. Michael kept apologizing and saying he hoped they had done the right thing. I couldn't thank him enough! The emotions I felt at that time were just incredible. And I never cried so much in my life! I was so happy for me, sad for my mother and scared at the same time. I was extremely upset that my mother had to go through an experience like that. It had to be the MOST difficult decision she ever made. Even now, when I think about how scared and alone she must have felt...it's heartbreaking. Not very much is known about the father, other than that little piece of information from Sarah. Pat was able to get a name from Sarah, but she wasn't really too sure about it. Pat says she has never really felt a need to find information on her father. She's curious, sure, but her main objective was to find her birth mother.

I have to admit I've gone through all my mother's pictures numerous times over the past couple years, looking for someone who looks like a "boxer." My mother was a great picture-taker and I have many, many pictures taken by her over the years. Many of the pictures have names and dates on the back (or in the scrapbooks). However, there seems to be a gap and I can't find any pictures taken between 1938 and 1940. Strange.

The next morning, I knew I had to tell the kids. Since Kristine lived only a couple blocks away, she was first. At that time, she had a "don't call before 10AM on weekends" rule. Being the considerate mother that I am, even though it was difficult, I waited to call at exactly 10AM and told her I was on my way over. Gwen lived 45 minutes away, so she had to settle for a phone call. They were as flabbergasted as I was! Gwen was 6 when her Grandma passed away and she had been *very* close to her, spending every weekday with her while her father and I worked. Kristine, unfortunately, was only 2 at the time, so she doesn't remember her Grandma at all, but she certainly could appreciate the story!

I also have to say that referring to my mother as Pat's "birth mother" sounds weird – better than "biological mother," but weird nonetheless. However, referring to her as Pat's mother isn't really right either. Pat was raised by a wonderful woman who was most definitely Pat's mother. So I guess "birth mother" it is.

Anyway, I e-mailed Pat, telling her that I had contacted a relative who had confirmed everything.

P At this point, I was careful to keep my contact with Michael to myself. I focused on the information that I had as well as the information that I had researched for myself, once I had been given supporting data from Michael.

As the communication with Arlene continued over the next few days, it was determined that we would like to meet. A face to face meeting would afford us the chance to ask and answer the questions that we each had. A date and time was set up and I counted the hours until 10 AM Saturday morning, in much the same way that a child counts the days, hours and minutes until their birthday, Christmas, or a vacation to Disney World.

A A couple days before Pat and I were to meet for the first time, my brother-in-law and his wife came over to visit. I, of course, had all kinds of happy news to tell them and they were very happy and excited for me. My sister-in-law and I had to go somewhere and decided, just for the heck of it, let's do a little "drive by" in Scotia (can you say "stalker?"). When we turned onto Pat's street and passed her house, I couldn't believe it! Her house looked just like mine! Cape Cod style, enclosed front porch. What were the odds of that?

P In our e-mails planning our first meeting, we addressed the obvious question of how would we recognize each other. The question itself sounds a little silly. Of course, we'd be the two people looking around for someone we didn't know. We did decide to say what we'd be wearing and that would certainly serve as identification.

Prior to the meeting of my little sister, I decided that I would like to have some small gift for her. I recalled that I would have been nearly eleven years old when she was born. What would an eleven-year-old child give her baby sister? A doll! Well that didn't seem to make much sense, but instead I selected a Willow Tree figurine – *Angel of Miracles*. It would be sort of a grownup doll, which truly expressed what this journey had been.

Aside from the butterflies in my stomach, I was ready for this moment that I have been looking forward to for so long. The mixture of emotions is hard to capture in words. There was the unspeakable JOY of meeting, for the first time in my life, a person to whom I was closely related by ties of blood. There was the fleeting thought of what we would do if this had not been a good idea. Then of course there was the human concern, would she like me?

I got into the car on the morning of November 15, 2008, and drove to the restaurant, carefully calculating my arrival to be about five to ten minutes early. I went up the steps and entered the small lobby of the restaurant and turned around to await Arlene's arrival. Just as I turned around to look out the door, a car pulled into the parking spot next to mine. There she was. My sister! We were mere seconds from meeting for the first time.

Once we greeted each other in a long and warm hug, the first thing I noticed was Arlene's brown eyes. Over a cup of coffee we began the process of sharing our stories. The stories of our lives, we found, were not that different. We were each raised as an only child. We had lived in reasonable proximity. And like me, Arlene admitted to having driven by my house, once she had the address. I guess we were alike in that, too.

One of her first comments to me, at the insistence of her daughters, was that there was no history of cancer or diabetes in the family, but that our mother had died at age 57 of heart disease. The latter fact, I had known from the death certificate, but her wisdom in letting me know of pertinent medical history overwhelmed me. Our mother had raised a sensitive, caring daughter.

Arlene told me of her life. She told stories that began to put a person and personality to the woman I had known only as "Elizabeth." From the start she seemed so at ease with referring to her mother as **our** mother. I learned of Arlene's family, her work (before retirement) and of her grandchildren.

Soon, it was obvious that we should order more than coffee, so we had a light breakfast. That was followed by lunch as noontime came and went.

As time went on, I told her of the family in which I was raised peopled by my parents and my many cousins. I spoke of attending Saint Joseph's Academy in downtown Schenectady and of our noontime forays to the shops and department stores. Our mother had worked at the Carl Company. We frequently went to Carl's. Did I ever see my mother? That is a question for which I will never have a definite answer.

Another piece of my history that I shared with Arlene was of the thirty years that I had spent as a Sister of Saint Joseph, ministering in the schools and parishes of the capital area as a member of the same religious congregation that had cared for me as an infant. It was during these years that I was assigned to teach at Immaculate

Conception School in the Bellevue section of Schenectady. During a five-year stretch of time we were living within blocks of each other. The questions come to mind: Did our paths ever cross? Did we see each other in the neighborhood stores?

Arlene was not raised in a Catholic family. As her mother explained it to her, she had been "thrown out of the Church" when she married Arlene's father, a divorced man. To this day, that statement haunts and hurts me. It always will. How could a person who had made such a courageous choice in life be excluded from a Church that preaches the care, compassion and forgiveness of a loving God. I know that the Church, my Church, does not permit divorce and remarriage unless there has been an annulment. My head understands the ruling, but my heart just cannot.

We talked for five hours straight that day. And so it has been in our subsequent meetings. We have two lifetimes to catch up on. The things I have been looking for I have found in my sister – brown eyes and straight hair and a wonderful friend.

A̲ The day we were to meet finally arrived and I was SO nervous! I had no idea what to expect. My biggest concern was that she would be angry. I know these things don't always end nicely and I don't know if I could have handled that. I hate confrontation of any kind but don't EVEN say anything mean about either of my parents (look what happened to my aunt while we were in Canada)! Plus, I knew I could easily get used to this idea of having a sister! Finally, at 58 years old, I had a SISTER! I just kept thinking, "Please, don't take this away from me now."

The minute I saw Pat, I knew all this was very real and I didn't need a DNA test to confirm it. She looked just like my mother – OUR mother! I always thought I looked like her, but I guess I must actually look more like my father. This was just unbelievable! One of my first questions to her was to ask if she had a good life. I was so scared about that. But, much to my relief, she told me she had a great life. She, too, was raised as an only child, but she grew up with many, many cousins nearby. We spent the next 5 hours talking, laughing and crying. I'm sure our waitress must have loved us, taking up a table all day, and I sure hope we tipped her well!

When Pat said she had "little information" leading her to believe that my mother was her birth mother, she wasn't being totally truthful. She started out with only her adoption certificate stating her name as Patricia Ann Morris and she always knew that her birth mother's name was Elizabeth Morris, who lived in the Glens Falls/Hudson Falls/Fort Edward area of New York State. Then she opened the binder she had brought with her! She went on to find that her birth mother had married Walter Richter, had another daughter, moved to Schenectady, New York, passed away in 1977 and was buried in Hudson Falls. She knew almost every place I ever lived and even had pictures of some of them! She knew where and when I graduated from high school, when I got married and where WE had lived!

One question Pat asked about our mother kind of stumped me. "What kind of person was she?" I had never really thought about it before. I stumbled around and finally said she was kind, happy, had a lot of friends – not much "real" information and I don't know why that question threw me. Of COURSE she would want to know this!

She was indeed "kind, happy and had a lot of friends." She

was also sarcastic (though NOT in a mean way), which I have seen in Pat, the same as I see it in myself (and my daughters). One time, while she was working as a waitress, she went from one restaurant to another when the owner changed. Many of her regular customers went with her. My mother-in-law, who worked with her at the first place, said she thought people followed her because they never knew what she was going to say next and didn't want to miss it.

She was also loving – none of us left the house without a kiss good-bye, even when just going to the store – and, before going to bed, it was kisses and hugs all around.

She cared very deeply about her friends and cried as easily as she laughed. This is one area where Pat differs. Although she laughs easily, she refuses to cry until no one is around. I, on the other hand, have been known to cry over coffee commercials at Christmas time.

One other likeness I have found between Pat and our mother is in the area of entertaining. Pat says she doesn't do it because she doesn't do it well. This is exactly something our mother would say. In reality, Pat does it **very** well, and so did our mother. One day, Pat invited me, along with 2 friends of ours, to her home for lunch. She had made a wonderful hot chicken salad and dessert consisted of an amazing meringue topped with berries. She is a great cook, even if she believes otherwise. Before we sat down to eat, our friends and I were sitting in the living room chatting while Pat put the finishing touches to the meal. One of our friends made the comment that Pat seemed really "wound up," meaning nervous or fretting over things. That's exactly the way our mother would get! I remember my husband asking me, early in our marriage, "Why does she get like that? No one cares if everything isn't **perfect**." No one but her (and Pat).

P   The first thing on my agenda the next morning was to send an e-mail to Michael to tell him of our meeting.

11/16/2008

Good Morning, Michael,

You may have already heard from Arlene, but I'll check in, too. We met and visited for 5 (FIVE) hours. It would be impossible to capture in words the emotions of joy, excitement, relief, etc., etc., etc., that we experienced in meeting for the first time.

While Arlene made several references to you, and the help you have been in connecting with her MORRIS side of the family; in meeting your Mother this summer; double checking with you when she got my letter, I did not give any indication that we had been in contact.

We will continue to get acquainted and BE sisters to each other. Next Sunday we are going up to Union Cemetery to "tell" Betty that we have found each other and that we are glad that she had two daughters. In case Arlene didn't send a picture, here is the one from my camera. Her's might be a little different- but not much.

Thank you for all that you did that made our meeting possible.

Pat

It was not long before I had Michael's reply.

11/16/2008

Hi Pat,

Yes, your e-mails were 43 minutes apart today, yours being the first and the only one with a picture. I am very glad everything is working out for both of you. Arlene was amazed at how much you resemble Betty. I must admit I did tear up slightly reading your e-mails and I know everything will be just great. Arlene really sounds so positive and really happy with finding you and finding a sister.

I'm also very happy for you, that your wait is over and the response is most excellent. I just know you two will be great, close sisters.

Take care,

Michael

P   Before leaving the restaurant, we set up a plan to visit the cemetery in Hudson Falls, NY, where our mother was buried. The date selected was the following Sunday. When I stopped at her home to pick Arlene up for our trip, I met her two daughters – my nieces. I also met her husband and mother-in-law who had known our mother. Her comment, "You look like your mother," both pleased and startled me. I had not yet become used to hearing that. As we traveled the hour long trip, we covered a lot more territory, literally and figuratively. The minutes and miles sped by, and soon we were at the cemetery.

As we stood, side by side, Arlene and I found peace in visiting our mother, sensing that, after all these years, she had her daughters together. The secret that must have burdened her throughout her life was no longer a shame or a secret. Rather it was an unbelievable, peaceful JOY. And all was well.

A The day we were to visit the cemetery, I wanted Pat to meet my husband, daughters and my mother-in-law, who was living with us at the time. I think I was as nervous about that as about anything else! Pat is, like me, somewhat shy and I didn't want her to feel overwhelmed. This whole journey had been overwhelming and I didn't want her to feel uncomfortable. Because of this, I think I hurried everything along. Kristine had gotten there first and, when Gwen arrived, I felt like I just introduced them and said "let's go." Maybe not, but that's how it felt later.

I was a bit nervous about going to the cemetery, too. Although I had been there many times throughout the years, I had never felt the "need" to go before, like I did now. I had always felt that my parents were in my heart, and I talked to them all the time. I didn't really need to drive for an hour to do the same thing. But now it felt different. I now felt it was important to go, with my sister, and let my mother know we were together, we were happy, and that Pat was very thankful to her for what she did for her.

P About a month later we decided to get together for dinner at the same restaurant that had been the scene of our first meeting. Christmas was fast approaching but there had been no reference to this being a "Christmas dinner." It had been determined that, in spite of having been invited to the holiday dinner at Arlene's, I would have to continue with the family tradition that had been a part of my life for many years. I would join my cousin and her family on Christmas. At the restaurant on that winter evening, we both arrived with gifts to exchange. It was amusing to note that each had selected a small, silver gift. Arlene gave me a bracelet with a silver heart, bearing my March birthstone on the front. It is inscribed on the back with the Chinese symbol for "Family." I had selected for Arlene a silver chain with a small pendant inscribed with the words: "A Sister is someone to laugh, sing, dance and cry with."

With only a month of being "Family," being "Sisters," it was clear that we shared a delight in this new-found relationship.

A My life since meeting my sister has been...unbelievable! My childhood wish has come true. Whenever she calls and Caller ID comes up on our TV (thank you, Time Warner), my husband yells out, "It's your sister." He's told me many times he loves saying that. Not as much as I love hearing it! For so long, because of losing contact with relatives, I felt like I had no family. I always had my husband's four brothers, their wives and children and my mother-in-law lived with us for a short while before she passed away in 2009, but it wasn't the same. Especially after hearing from Michael and getting all the information he had on the Morris side of the family, I felt something missing. I really had no background. Now I have my very own sister! And we're learning about our family together.

P The fascination with having a sister took many forms over the first several months of our acquaintance. It took a while for me to get used to saying the simple phrase,

"My sister and I ..." when referring to things we were doing together. It was not until several weeks later that I realized that everything referring to her family was firmly rooted in Arlene. When talking about her husband, Bruce, I found myself saying Arlene's husband. Her daughters were referred to in the same way, Arlene's daughters. Her grandsons, likewise, were identified as, just that. Suddenly it came to me. These people had a special relationship to me also. In gaining a sister, I had also expanded my family to include a brother-in-law, two nieces and two grand-nephews.

The family in which I was raised cherished their strong Irish Catholic faith and tradition. This has set forth the background against which I have formed my attitude and approach to my adoption. I never doubted or questioned the love my parents had for me. I was loved and cared for from the moment they took me into their home. I was given a good education, had a close circle of friends and enjoyed being a part of this family.

That said, I had a constant awareness of the fact that there was another piece of my life story that I thought would never be known to me. And so I entered into my own fantasies about the circumstances of my birth. I had conjured up a young girl of perhaps 15 or 16 who was not ready to forfeit her childhood for the burdens of motherhood. Nor would she have been ready to support a new young life, and so she made the decision to give her child the opportunity for a life in a mature family. Since so much of my life was faith-based, I selected, July 26, the feast of Saint Ann (mother of Mary, the mother of Jesus) as a day of remembrance for the mother I didn't know. Each year I would remember Elizabeth in a special way on that day. There were three other dates on which the impact of Elizabeth's decision have been remembered with gratitude dating back to before my junior high school days. Those were, and still are, my birthday, Mother's Day and the anniversary of my adoption, December 30.

Listening to the scriptures found within the annual cycle of readings in our Catholic liturgy, when I would hear a passage from Isaiah it would raise a question in my mind. The following are the words from the Book of Isaiah, Chapter 49 verse 15.

"Can a woman forget her nursing child or show no tenderness for the child of her womb?

Even these may forget, yet I (God) will not forget you."

Did Elizabeth forget me? That thought has tormented me through the years. She had become a real part of my life even though we would never meet. Yet, the thought that she may have erased all memory of my existence hurt in some strange way. Nor did I want her tormented by that memory or by the question of my well-being. I had no way of knowing for sure. It was truly a complex mental process for me. It was one I struggled with for years. Those anxieties released their grip the day I read the wedding announcement for Arlene PATRICIA Richter. I grasped that as a sure sign that, indeed, I had not been forgotten. Eleven years after my birth, my name was passed on when Elizabeth had another daughter. In all that had been revealed over the past year, that simple discovery had the deepest, instant emotional effect.

Who would have thought that selecting a greeting card would present a challenge? For the first time in my life I was looking for a Christmas card for my *sister*. The beautiful cards carried various sentiments for a happy holiday. Keep in mind that I had only known my sister for about a month when I struggled to select a card designed for My Sister and Brother-in-law. Most cards made reference to previous years. We had no previous years. We had no history together that would be reflected in the celebrations of holidays like Christmas. Other cards seemed cold, perhaps designed for the obligatory greeting between family members who were not especially close. None of these seemed to say the appropriate things for our situation.

This dilemma carried on to finding a birthday card the following March. I think I read every card in the shop, trying to find a message that was warm and sincere, but not referring to growing up together, old memories and childish squabbles. In both cases a somewhat suitable card was found and as we discussed the quandary the selection posed for us, we found that we both had been in the same dilemma.

A I think it's rather ironic that my birthday, Pat's birthday and our mother's birthday are all in March. However, finding birthday and holiday cards is a time-consuming task. Our situation is not normal. I have to say, I think Pat has it a little easier than me. One of her talents is making note cards using photographs she has taken. She could, and has, put beautiful, heartfelt thoughts on one of her beautiful photos while I, on the other hand, must search out something that makes sense for us. And these are few and far between. You would think Hallmark would have thought of this by now. Do they have a suggestion box?

P As the days and weeks moved on, we found our life stories being gently unfolded. I was being given a ringside seat from which to view the life of my birth mother. Arlene had told me that she had an old 8mm movie that would show her mother at a backyard gathering. Since neither of us had an 8mm projector, she arranged to have it transferred to a DVD for viewing with our contemporary equipment. The day came when she brought the DVD and we popped it into the player. As we watched the segment leading up to the appearance of her mother, I became aware that she was watching for my reaction. The image of the mother I had never known was on the screen, but for a moment. It was hard to absorb the impact of seeing her as a living, moving person. I think I disappointed my sister, by not showing any visible emotion. There were too many dynamics in play for me to sort out in that instant. It was a powerful experience and I was, to all appearances, numb to it.

This was but one of many times when I felt a deep, emotional reaction to a piece of the process of our getting to know each other. But expressing the intensity of my feelings, in the presence of others, has always been a major hang-up of mine. Alone, there is no stopping the tears that well up and flow like Niagara. That can happen in the quiet of my home or driving down the street when an especially touching, beautiful or sad thought travels across the landscape of my consciousness. Arlene on the other hand can easily give way to her emotions. I think this is one of the most obvious characteristics in which we differ. I want to be just like my little sister "when I grow up." For her sake and for mine.

A Watching Pat while she watched the video of our mother was fascinating. She said she had no "visible emotion," but just because she didn't cry doesn't mean I didn't see her emotion. She was totally wrapped up in seeing this video and the look on her face was one of –

amazement, for lack of a better word. Although she had seen still pictures of her, a video is completely different. My mother didn't like having her picture taken, so she was always the "picture taker," rarely in pictures herself. This was one time I was the one with the camera and, when she looked at the camera, you could read her lips when she said," That's enough." But it *was* enough. Pat got to see her as a living, breathing person.

P   At one point, talking of her young life, Arlene asked if I would like to see the pictures from her wedding. Of course I would! I jumped at the offer by responding, "Yes, I really would. After all, I wasn't invited to the wedding." That quick quip evoked a reaction I had not expected. Arlene seemed, visibly, to be upset by having this pointed out, though in jest. It was at that moment I realized how sensitive Arlene was to the illusion of "guilt." Of course there was no way she could have invited me. She didn't even know I existed. There was not an ounce of responsibility that could be assigned to her for the oversight. Being a Big Sister, I now had a point that I could use for some sibling teasing. All in moderation and clearly identified as in a spirit of jest, of course.

Seeing the lovely young bride and her husband on their wedding day was the next best thing to being there. There were the pictures of Arlene with her mother, and with her father and with the friends she had gathered around to share her special day. Now, in a strange way I, too, was able to be included in spite of the forty-plus year time lapse.

P   *Getting to know you. Getting to know all about you.* This was to become the theme of the next few months. I had already met Arlene's immediate family. There were many more people to whom she wanted to introduce me and I certainly wanted her to meet my family.

I had received a beautiful letter at Christmas from her sister-in-law, Judy, who lives in Florida. It carried the warm message of "welcome to the family." That was followed by a promise to meet the following summer, when they came up North for their annual visit.

Then in January, Arlene's mother-in-law, Martha, died after a brief illness. I knew that she had been in failing health and sensed that death was near from Arlene's reports. But I was stunned when I received a phone call from another sister-in-law, Joni, stating that Martha had died about an hour earlier and she thought that Arlene needed to talk to me. Me? We had only met a month and a half earlier. How could I be the one she needed at such a time? I was happy to be called on to be a part of Arlene's support system at this time of very personal loss.

As I approached the side door of the funeral home for Martha's wake, a man standing on the porch said, "You must be Pat." Well, I couldn't deny it. But who was he? The awkward moment collapsed in an instant when he introduced himself as Chuck, Bruce's brother. He had obviously heard about me. Once inside, I also met Chuck's wife, Judy, from whom I had received the lovely Christmas letter. With very little time to think about the course of events, I met Bruce's three brothers and their wives. At Martha's wake, Arlene's daughters (my nieces) brought their friends and introduced them to their *aunt*. This was also the first time that I saw my grand-nephews, Luke and Ben, as well as several of Arlene's friends. Now there were faces to attach to the names that had come up as we talked of our families. How would I ever keep it all straight?

A Pat was so surprised that someone would "recognize" her, which is exactly what happened when my brother-in-law, Chuck, saw her. He knew our mother and, as I keep telling Pat, she looks just like her. She has told me that she never knew anyone who looked like her and doesn't know how to see the similarities, but her resemblance to our mother is uncanny – same hair, same eyes, same mouth. And it's still strange to see a picture of us together and realize we're standing the same way, or smiling the same way. I think we have the same laugh and my daughters say we have the same hands!

P But this was a two-way street. I had a close family of cousins who had delighted in my news of finding

Arlene. I wanted so much, for them to meet Arlene and for her to meet them. In June, I had a family picnic for the express purpose of bringing about this meeting. My cousin Ray and his wife Jacquie came down from Warrensburg. Ray's sister, Gail came in from Binghamton. Two cousins who live in the Scotia area arrived.

While this was only a sampling of my extended family, it did offer Arlene a small look into the family that has been mine. These cousins had been my playmates in childhood, and friends in adulthood. It was a surprise when my cousin, Kathy, recognized Arlene's husband, Bruce. They had been co-workers at the *Daily Gazette*. Small world, isn't it? To add to the coincidence, Kathy had worked at the Carl Company and remembered Betty from the lunch counter in the store. She knew and remembered my mother and I never knew her and so could not remember.

Then on the Fourth of July I planned to make my annual trip to visit cousins in the Hartford area of Connecticut.

Spending the patriotic holiday with these relatives is a tradition that dates back forty-some years. I invited Arlene to go with me so that the folks there would have the joy of meeting my sister, too. It was a wonderful day and an old tradition took on a new dimension that included my sister.

A   Now it was my turn to meet her family. I don't think I was as nervous or apprehensive as she had been on meeting my family. By this time, maybe 7 months after our initial meeting, I was comfortable enough with Pat and knew that, since they were all raised together and remained friends, they would probably be as nice as she was – plus the fact that my husband was with me might have helped, too! But I was right – they were indeed very, very nice people and I was very happy to be included in their family. And it was strange, to say the least, when my husband recognized one of Pat's cousins from when he worked at the _Daily Gazette_! It makes you realize what a small world this is and makes us wonder how many times our paths may have crossed!

Pat had put together a small booklet that told, very briefly, of our journey so far and gave each of her cousins a copy. It was awesome to watch them read it – each and every one of them cried!!

P In the short time that we have merged our lives into one family, many events have been a part of the process. My birthday, for example, was the occasion for starting a new tradition. Arlene and Bruce invited me to a birthday dinner. For my first 50 birthdays, I had shared the day and the celebration with my mother, Marguerite. It had always been a family day of gathering. Aunts, uncles and cousins would arrive on our mutual birthday evening with best wishes and gifts. Since her death, in 1990, I had the day to myself. I had always made it a point to stay in that evening, to be there when my cousins called from out of town. They were very faithful about acknowledging my birthday, and I in turn, tried to check in on theirs. But in 2009 I accepted the invitation and went to my sister and brother-in-law's house for dinner. It was the beginning of a new tradition; our own traditions had begun. The cousins caught on to the fact that they would have to call the night before.

We both soon realized that we had holiday celebrations and traditions within our families which needed to be honored and maintained. We found ourselves creating new ways to observe special days in a new way.

Starting at Easter and Christmas of that same year, I was invited to join Arlene's family for brunch. As the extended family joined in holiday celebrations, I had been absorbed into it. I felt welcomed and quite at home in the new circumstance. Now this might seem to need no explanation, to many. For me, it was completely out of character. I find new situations and meeting groups of new people to be quite difficult. This blending of families has not been that way for me. There is no angst or distress in anticipation of an event. There has been only joyous expectation and delight in participation in these family gatherings. At a recent Christmas it was expanded to Christmas Eve dinner with my niece, Gwen, and her family. Each event seems to have a special moment that is touching and tender. On Christmas Eve, as we sat in the family room after dinner, six-year-old Ben, took me by the hand and said "Aunt Pat, I want to show you something." Not only was Ben my grand-nephew, but he called me AUNT Pat. I'm getting used to hearing it, but each time it has such a beautiful sound.

Oh, and what was it that Ben just had to show me? The calendar on the refrigerator clearly indicated that *tomorrow* would be Christmas. Nothing could be more exciting to a six –year-old. And nothing could be more exciting to me, than that he wanted me to know it, and he called me "aunt" in the process.

Added to our own unique traditions is the annual celebration of our meeting day, November 15th. This is a day with no competition in category of Hallmark-days. It does not require a greeting card. It is truly *our* day. It only requires that we get together and share the joy that has been ours as we count the years.

In July of 2010 we were invited to celebrate Sarah's 90th birthday. The gathering would be at the home of Michael's brother, Bill, and his wife. We were both excited to be a part of such a special family event. We were a little nervous, too. We would be meeting a large group of cousins, their spouses and children. All had heard our story from Sarah and Michael. Our fears were quickly put to rest by the warm welcome we received and the total inclusion in the festivities. It was a wonderful party, celebrating the life of a woman we had come to know and love.

In the Fall of 2010, the Loucks family had arranged to have a family portrait taken. It would include their extended family, right down to Jake, the Boston terrier. Surprisingly, they asked me to be a part of the sitting. I have never been in a family portrait. My family, as I was growing up, didn't have any pictures taken that included the three of us. We have plenty of pictures of us, but never together. This would be a first for me. When we gathered at the studio, it was amusing to note that Arlene and I had worn sweaters that were identical – her's in white and mine in blue. Having been invited to be a part of the Family Portrait was just one more affirmation of my having been drawn into this wonderful family.

Family Portrait – November 13, 2010

A When we first started talking about writing a book, and I mentioned that I did love to write, she said, "I know...you were in Ebenwyck in high school." What? Ebenwyck? What's that? Apparently it was a writing club of some kind. She sent me a picture from my high school yearbook and there I was...in Ebenwyck. I must not have been in it for very long (or just showed up for picture day), as I have absolutely no memory of it whatsoever! Ahhhh....the sixties. I meant the 1960's but just realized that I'm 60, so.... Anyway... I just can't imagine how Pat felt when she found my wedding announcement and, in huge letters over my picture, it said, "Arlene Patricia Richter Weds Bruce A. Loucks." When did anyone ever put a headline like *that* in the paper? I like to think, and I hope Pat does, too, that I was given her name on purpose, in essence, making sure we were all together. Which brings me to questions.

There are so many questions:

How did Pat know her birth mother's name and where she was from? Obviously, she got that information from her mother, but how did her mother know? Unlike today, with "open" adoptions where everyone knows everyone else and the birth mother can even have visitation rights, adoptions were very secret. No one, including the child, knew anything. Then, at the "appropriate" time, they would sit the child down and tell them that their whole life was not what it had seemed. According to any TV show I've seen where one character turned out to have been adopted – and it only happened on TV, as far as I knew – they were always told, "We CHOSE you." That's actually kind of nice.

Did my mother name Pat? She always thought she was named Patricia because her birthday is the day before St. Patrick's Day. But if my mother hadn't named her, she surely must have known the name given to her because I think it's *too* much of a coincidence that Patricia is my middle name.

Why did we end up living in Schenectady, just 10 minutes from where Pat was in Scotia? My father was from Connecticut, my mother was from upstate New York. They met in Bridgeport, Connecticut, and were married in Glens Falls, NY. I was born in Glens Falls, then we moved to Stillwater, NY, back to Connecticut for a while, then to Schenectady. By that time, I was all of 5 years old. Although we moved to Colonie, NY, for about a year (when I was 7), which is between Albany and Schenectady, we were back in Schenectady by the time I was 8 years old. We did move several times after that, but we always stayed in Schenectady. I often wondered why we ended up here – it wasn't that my father worked at the biggest employer in the area, General Electric, and they moved here to be closer to his job. My father actually had quite a few jobs, none of which involved the GE. He was a police officer in Bridgeport, Connecticut. When they moved to Glens Falls, he began driving a taxi then drove Trailways buses for a while. I have no idea whatsoever what he did when we lived in Connecticut, but he began driving buses for Schenectady Transportation when we moved here. It seems that he would have found a job no matter where we lived, so…why here? Pat thought maybe they were getting away from family who may have known about that first baby, wanting to keep that information away from me. However, I knew a lot of my mother's relatives – we saw other cousins of my mother's quite often and my aunt and uncle must *definitely* have known – there never seemed to be any worry about someone saying something that I would overhear.

People have asked me if I thought my father knew about Pat. I have to say I think he did. My parents went through a lot together, including a near break-up because my father missed his kids and then my father resigning from the Bridgeport Police Department because, believe it or not, the Department didn't like the fact that he was dating while he was only separated from his wife – they had even sent a representative to my mother's apartment who told her to leave town! Can you imagine something like that happening today? Plus, the fact that he was married before and had 2 children would lead me to believe it would have been fairly easy for my mother to tell him about her child. I also have to believe my father knew because it hurts too much to think my mother was holding this fact inside, feeling she couldn't tell anyone.

P   Throughout this process there is an underlying concern. It is the question of my fidelity to and loyalty toward the family that raised me, my nurturing family.

They took me in, unconditionally. They loved me when I was quite unlovable. You know, those teen years! They nursed me through measles, mumps and chicken pox. They sought care for my broken arm and bandaged many a skinned knee. They encouraged me in my interests whether it was Girl Scouting, bicycling or amateur photography at a very young age. My parents provided me with a good, solid schooling, through to a Bachelors Degree in Education. Our many family outings and travels had given me a broad view of this world in which we live. Truly they had made all the sacrifices and choices that they felt were for my good. I had a wonderful life thanks to my parents, John and Marguerite.

Now, I have become a member of another family. I have embraced this new life with joy. Then, suddenly, I am stopped short in my tracks. Am I turning away from my other family? Can I be a full fledged member of both families? Is it selfish of me to be so invested in my new identity? These are questions that arise, but do not disturb my inner peace. At times it seems as though my head is spinning, as I try to comprehend all that has happened over the past couple of years.

At the time of the picnic for my cousins, I presented each with a small account of our meeting and it concluded with this statement.

> "I have not submitted a "resignation" from the family in which I was raised. I was informed that it would be rejected, if submitted. Instead, you, my cousins have enthusiastically shared in my happiness and I am so happy to introduce you to Arlene. She is a wonderful addition to my life and to our family."

Limitations of Language

Words can become a stumbling block or an interesting vehicle of communication. This has become evident as we struggle to find a word for what has happened to Arlene and me. We cannot really refer to it as a reunion. <u>Webster's New World Dictionary</u> defines it this way:

Re-un'-ion n. 1. a coming together again, as after separation.

We have not been reunited. What is it then? Meeting? Connecting? Encounter? These words seem too clumsy, and do not really carry the impact of the experience. So we continue to struggle with finding a suitable word to use.

There is also the duel between the concept of ancestry and heritage. I have come to believe that people who have been born and raised in a family, will find that these two words can almost be used interchangeably. Again, let's look to Webster for definitions:

An'-ces-try n. 1. family descent 2. all ones ancestors

Her'-it-age n. 1. Property that is or can be inherited 2. a tradition handed down from the past

In the case of a child who is adopted, the ancestry, the blood line, comes from the birth family. This will be reflected in eye, skin and hair color; stature; predisposition to disease; and to some extent, mannerisms. It was this incongruity with my adoptive family that caused strangers to note that I "must have been adopted" since I did not resemble the family in which I was growing up.

Heritage, on the other hand, comes from the environment in which one is raised. It can include the way holidays are celebrated or the china from which the holiday meals are eaten. One's heritage may be the Faith of the family or the values placed on work or education. In some cases the heritage may include language and food. Heritage is made up of the day to day life within the nurturing family. Carrying it to the logical conclusion, heritage is the legacy, including material things that are passed onto a child when the parents die.

There is the legal aspect of the adoption which creates a bond between the adoptive parents and the adopted child. In my adoption papers, it clearly states, ". . . husband and wife, have duly agreed to adopt said child and to make her their own lawful child. They herby agree to raise the child as their own, without the distinction of adoption, and pass along to the child the heritage, customs and values of their family."

That phrase, "without the distinction of adoption," is perhaps the reason that I was never sure of how much of my status coming into this family was known by my cousins. While there was never a time when I was not aware of having been adopted, it was not an issue which was discussed in the family, especially the extended family. As my cousins grew to adulthood it is not surprising that their parents would have told them. How or in what context the revelation was made, I do not know. It is not important to me.

Although I had spent many years in genealogical research of my adoptive family, it was not until I had access to my birth family records that I had a glimpse into my ancestry.

This dissecting of the words *ancestry* and *heritage* is purely my interpretation of these words. It was a distinction that I felt I had to make for my own use. It in no way diminishes or negates the influence of my adoptive family. They are the ones who have formed and molded me into the woman I have become. The search to find and know of my birth family was not a search to "find out who I am." I know who I am. The person I have become is the direct result of all of my life experiences. My nurturing family has given me a Faith foundation to live by; values to adhere to; traditions to observe; family to love and be loved by in return. They gave me experiences of travel and education, supported me in joys and sorrows. This is my heritage.

A final problem that I have with language is the commonly used term, *birth mother*. To me it seems to be so clinical (but not as bad a biological mother). In fact, Elizabeth Morris was my mother at birth. *Legally*, she terminated her claim to the relationship of mother when she signed the release papers. But in my life, her decision did not relinquish our connection. She gave me life. That is the role of a mother. That is a strong bond. To use the term birth mother, to me is akin to fingernails on a chalk board. So rather than try to choose between Marguerite and Betty, I prefer to think that I have been doubly blessed. I truly have two mothers. Both have earned the title; each in a different way. Both have fulfilled their duties to their child. Another attempt is often made to distinguish the child of adopting parents. I have never thought of my nurturing parents as my *adoptive parents*. Legally, there is no need for noting and naming them according to that fact. Referring back to my legal papers, it clearly states that the parents, "agree to raise the child (me) as their own." Truly, I was theirs and they were mine. No apology or explanation was necessary.

Michael

P In the nearly two years of my communication with Michael, he had made it quite clear that he did not want me to reveal, to Arlene, the fact that we had been in contact. I fully understood his thought. He feared that it would seem that his reaching out to Arlene for genealogical information was some sort of covert process, done to provide me with information. He did not want to offend her or jeopardize the relationship they were building.

In the days and weeks following our November meeting, Arlene and I were getting together regularly and growing in our knowledge and understanding of each other. We were each updating Michael of our activities together. Then things began to get a little dicey.

At one point Michael asked me to send him the picture he had so graciously given me a year and a half earlier. He said he would have two copies made up. He planned to send them to Arlene, who could then share one with me. I decided to save Michael the trouble of having the copies made, so I sent him the original plus two copies which I had printed on my computer.

In a matter of a couple of weeks, enclosed with her Christmas card from Mike, Arlene received the two pictures of her mother. She was happy to share one with me, as directed by Mike. Unknown to her, each time she came to my house I had had to stow away a copy of that very picture, lest I betray the Mike connection.

In early January, I had invited Arlene to supper. At this time she was bringing pictures for me to scan and add to my collection of the MORRIS ALBUM on my computer. As the conversation went on, she was telling me of things her cousin in Florida was sharing with her. It was getting to be quite humorous. Arlene was telling me anecdotal stories of this cousin in Florida. They were stories that I had heard directly from Mike. Finally it came to the point where I could not continue with the charade. I felt very strongly that we could not establish a viable relationship with this secret as a crumbling block in the foundation. I knew this moment had to come. Finally I just said to Arlene that I had, indeed, been in contact with Michael for nearly two years. By this time, I knew that there was no reason to fear her reaction. Once the truth was out, we had a good laugh at the pretense that had caused such anxiety for me.

A   When Pat told me she had something to tell me, my heart skipped a beat. Although I had absolutely no idea what it could possibly be, and no reason to think it would be unpleasant, why do I always think it has to be something bad? She said she had been in contact with Michael for 2 years. Whew! Is that it? I was too relieved to be upset! I wouldn't have been upset anyway. I do understand Michael's point of not wanting me to think his contact with me was only for the purpose of finding out what I knew. Technically it may have been, but in this kind of situation, *someone* has to ask questions. Pat had gone as far as she could without actually contacting me with this information. She had no idea if this sister she found knew anything about her and, if so, how did she feel about it? She needed someone to "feel out" the situation – I can certainly understand that! The "unease" I felt on the day we met was *nothing* compared to what she must have felt during this entire quest. But I also realize that, at this point, Michael didn't really know me that well and didn't know what to expect if I found out his involvement. I could not then, and I cannot now, thank him enough!!

P When Arlene went home she e-mailed Michael, who in turn e-mailed me, saying it was better all around that the truth was out in the open.

The whole episode surrounding the secrecy of Michael's key role in our meeting seems funny now. Without his part in the research, I would never have known of the migration of our mother, her husband and their daughter from the North Country to the Schenectady area. I cannot adequately express the gratitude I have for Michael and his dear mother, Sarah. They are, truly, responsible for this joyous phase of my life and for the blending of our lives as sisters. We have both told them repeatedly of our gratitude.

Sharing

P I find myself wanting to introduce Arlene to all the important people in my life; to saturate all the places that are significant to me with her presence. How can this be done? Can it be done without making her uneasy? It is almost like adding her to all the dimensions of my life and allowing them to take on a completely new look. To make an analogy to illustrate I would compare it to a painter who has prepared a can of paint and then dropped a new tint into it. In an instant the entire quantity has taken on a new look. Every drop of paint has become something completely new and will never be returned to its former shade. It is new and bright and fresh. And that is how my life has been since Arlene has been added to it.

There was a dear friend of mine, a Sister of St. Joseph, who was suffering from a form of dementia. Since our friendship spanned more than 40 years, she was like a member of my family. My frequent visits to her in the healthcare facility at the community Motherhouse were an important part of my routine. I spoke to her of Arlene and had our picture hung in her room. I felt very strongly that I wanted these special people to know each other. On returning from a trip to Glens Falls, I asked Arlene if she would mind stopping to meet Sister Ann. Of course, she graciously said it would be fine. And so we did.

By a strange coincidence Sister Ann's mother was a Loucks, Arlene's last name. Subsequent genealogical research indicates that several generations back there may be a connection between Sister Ann's family and Arlene's husband's family.

It was not many months later that I asked Arlene if she would accompany me to the wake for Sister Ann. Her presence by my side at such a time of grief was a source of strength, beyond belief.

There is a Retreat Center in the Adirondack Mountains of New York that has figured prominently in my life over the last fifty-plus years. As a child I went to Marian Lodge, a Catholic camp for girls. It was located on Pyramid Lake, between Schroon Lake and Ticonderoga. Over the years it was transformed into Pyramid Life Center, hosting retreats throughout the summer months. There is also an annual "reunion" weekend for the former campers of Marian Lodge. Thus we celebrate the friendships formed over a half a century ago. So it was important to me that Arlene become a part of this setting. In the Fall of 2010, added to a visit to Sarah, we took the trip an hour further North so that Arlene could see just why I find it to be such a special place.

Another time, I had to make a quick trip to Warrensburgh to visit my cousins, Ray and Jacquie. The purpose for the trip was to take pictures which would become note cards for Jacquie to sell in a gift shop. I wanted the pictures to reflect the local area. Since it was to be a round trip visit I invited Arlene to join me. Ray is a Board member for the North Creek Railroad Museum. I knew he would give us a full scale tour of the museum and near-by Gore Mountain as I snapped pictures for my project. This again was a case of wanting Arlene to be a part of that part of my life. Although my sister had met Ray and Jacquie at the picnic, this was her first visit to their cabin.

Joint Ventures

Craft Fairs & Writing

We have begun joining up for other activities and shared interests. In the fall of 2009 we attended a village-wide craft fair in Middleburgh, NY. At that time we discussed the possibility of entering into a craft adventure together. Pat is a photographer, specializing in scenes of nature and creation. These are put together as note cards and matted prints. Arlene's love of candles transitioned to candle-making. It just made sense to "make scents." This, by the way, is something our mother enjoyed doing and Pat also did it at one time.

Our first event was held in the Fall of 2010, at a small Presbyterian Church in Charlton, NY. The experience was exciting, as we were introduced to a small group of crafters and launched into our new business with gusto. A small sign identifies our business as *Sister Act*. How appropriate! As the Fall continued, we were participants in several other events. Most were church-sponsored, or benefitted a school or a charity. Thus far it has been great fun, if not all that profitable.

At a craft fair in December of 2010, as we were looking for our space, to set up, Arlene asked what number we were looking for and Pat responded, "F-8." Arlene said, "Oh, fate." We got a little chuckle over that, since it was fate that brought us together.

Our business uniforms are blue tee shirts with the inscription, "My sister has the best sister in the world." We have found that this attracts attention from other vendors and customers. There are always questions about whether or not we are really sisters. Often our story unfolds as we explain our relationship.

As we were setting up, our shirts caught the eye of another vendor, who said she just had to tell us how great she thought they were. We talked for a few minutes about our business and asked her about what it was she did. She said she was an author and was there with her latest book. We looked at each other, shocked. Finally! Someone who might know what our first step should be. We told her very briefly about our journey and that, at the urging of friends and family who found the story to be worth telling, we were interested in putting it into print.

That was when she said she was also a publisher and was at the craft fair with information on workshops that she and her husband conduct to assist aspiring authors. She is also a motivational speaker in the field of writing for publication. Together with her husband, they own a publishing company. Our conversation affirmed our idea of putting our story into print. It also gave us the impetus to begin the task.

During our second year on the craft fair circuit, we met a young woman who was selling skin care products. In conversation, she told us of a co-op venture that featured nearly a hundred vender booths. It is like a continual craft fair. At her suggestion, we visited Artique in Clifton Park, NY. After wandering around the vast area of the business and making note of the various craft items that were featured, we decided to inquire about renting a space. The conditions of the rental required a monthly fee, based on the square footage of the space and 12 hours of service as a shop-keeper per month. We discussed it briefly and decided to jump in with both feet. Our space is the smallest in area in the shop. It suits our products just fine. We were to "move in" on May 1. Our immediate task was to find the display units. Arlene found a small unit of shelves and Pat purchased old louvered doors from ReStore, a service of Habitat for Humanity. The doors were then spray painted to match Arlene's shelves and we were set to go. The other co-op members are friendly and welcoming of newcomers to the business as well as to the customers. It is truly, "a unique shopping experience," as their business card reads. Sales have started out slowly, but we are optimistic that they will pick up once people know of our work. We shamelessly tell our friends of this venture and many have visited and made purchases from our booth and from others in the store.

Bicycle Riding

We have also begun bike riding together, although we don't get to do that as much as we would like. Since we missed out on many of the fun things of a childhood together, we decided to do some of the things that might have been done back in the day. Keep in mind that there is an eleven year difference in our ages. So for the big sister to have had to take her little sister out bike riding might have been done only under duress at the time. We decided that at our ages, the exercise value would be good for both of us. There is a beautiful bike trail that follows the bank of the Mohawk River from Schenectady County Community College to Rotterdam Junction. It is a gentle ride. There are just enough hills to keep the heart pumping. As we peddled and talked or stopped and rested, we continued to be amazed at the miracle of "sisterhood." Our aim was to ride a couple of times a week. This worked the first summer. The second summer was not at all weather friendly. Either the heat was overpowering or the rain torrential. So our good intentions remained just that.

Mother's Day

As our first Mother's Day approached it seemed a new tradition was about to begin. We decided that the Saturday before Mother's Day would be an ideal time to travel, again, to the cemetery. Coupled with this visit was a stop at the Adult Home where Sarah McCall resides. Each time we drop in on her, we hear more stories of the "olden days." The stories she tells of the times she shared with our Mother gives life and personality to the person I (Pat) never knew. This annual journey has become one of the traditions that is uniquely ours.

Further Coincidences

As we talked of our lives and experiences, we soon realized that in strange ways the paths of our lives had similarities, if not actual points of crossing. One time we made parallel lists of when and where we had lived. This was simply an activity to get a feel for where we had been, but it revealed some interesting facts:

Arlene was born in Glens Falls in 1950 and lived there until 1953. Pat taught in Glens Falls during the 1967-68 school year.

In 1974 Pat Lived on Park Avenue in Albany, while Arlene

lived on Park Place in Schenectady.

1982 through 1985, both Pat and Arlene lived in Bellevue, Schenectady.

For a period of approximately 6 years, Arlene lived on Robinson Street in Schenectady. It was on the corner of Robinson & State Streets that Pat's Grandfather Flanigan had owned and operated a newsroom for many years. Although the years did not coincide, the fact that the location figured into both families was found to be amusing.

In conversation one day, during a spell of strange weather patterns in our area another connecting fact was revealed. Arlene mentioned that at the time of the tornado that passed through the Schenectady area in 1960, she was on a bus trip to New York City with her Girls Scout troop. The news of the tornado was told to the troop leader as they exited the New York State Thruway. Responding to the leader's nearly hysterical reaction, the bus load of little girls followed suit.

Pat, on the other hand was traveling home from a summer trip to Georgia with some of her college classmates. The four young women had been teaching in a summer school program at Saint Francis deSales Church in Brunswick, Georgia. The mother of one of the girls had gone down South to drive them home. During an especially heavy storm in the Wilmington, Delaware area they pulled over to await some let up of the pounding rain. As they listened to a very crackly report on the car radio they could just barely make out the announcement of a "tornado. . . Schenectady . . . heavy damage."

While we both were not exactly in the same place at the same time, we were both away from home and we both were getting the news in unusual ways during the same event.

Now what are the chances of this happening? One morning this past Fall, I walked as I always do, to the kitchen. Nothing has changed in the kitchen. No furniture has been moved or added. But somehow I walked into the leg of a chair. It was not long before I realized that I had broken the little toe on my left foot. Yes, that detail is important. I hobbled around the house, iced the toe and splint-bandaged it to the next toe. Later in the day I heard from Arlene that, while shopping, she had jammed her toe into the wheel of the shopping cart while wearing flip-flops. They did not provide the protection that would have prevented injury. I should have had slippers on. She should have worn shoes. We both broke the same toe on the same foot on the same day. Now what are the chances....?

Now when something like this happens or we do or say something similar the comment will be made, "It must be in the genes."

Sister Training

Pat had a long-time friend, Maryanne. She and her sister, Carolynn had taken a great interest in the story of our lives and meeting. It was not long until, in jest, we suggested that Maryanne and Carolynn be our mentors in how to be sisters. This has been an exciting relationship. What we have found in watching them and applying to our own interaction is that fun and laughter are key elements in their lives and ours. Although they were raised together and have shared a home for many years of their adulthood, they are true friends. Times shared with them are filled with laughter, and usually food. Food is a good glue for friendship. Carolynn is an excellent cook and meals hosted by them are delightful occasions. We have also gone together to dinners and other events. Maryanne and Carolynn made a lengthy journey to support us at our first craft fair. They have also been strong advocates of our sharing our story in print. What started out as a joke has become a reality. They are showing us the best parts of being sisters and sharing our joy in the process.

A Niece's Visit

P Shortly before Christmas, Arlene called to ask if I could re-size and format some pictures for Kris for a gift project she was doing. Since this is a part of my work with the card making, it was not a stretch to say an immediate "Yes" to the request. It can be truly stated that I was delighted to have been asked. Arlene e-mailed the photos to me and I replied shortly that they were done and printed. What happened next hit emotional buttons on so many levels. She said that Kris would be right over to pick them up. Kris had never been to my house before. This had not been a deliberate oversight, there had just never been an occasion. Suddenly I was overwhelmed by the piece that had been missing from my life. I had not been a part of my nieces' lives as Gwen and Kris were growing up. We hadn't had "girls days" when we could make cookies and cocoa together. Or perhaps go shopping and "do lunch" when they were young. Or hear the tales and secrets of their school days. These were the stories I had heard other aunts tell as they watched their nieces and nephews grow up. Again I was feeling the loss of a big chunk of what might have been.

But trying not to focus on the loss, I looked forward to my niece coming for her first, though brief, visit. How I wished the moment could have lasted longer. It was long enough, though, to hear the excited story of her purchase that morning of a Christmas gift for her mother. I had to promise not to tell my sister that her husband would be giving her a lap-top computer for Christmas. To me that moment, sharing that secret, was an aunt/niece moment that made up for those we had been denied all these years.

What's in a Name?

P   The word mother is a word like no other. It speaks of love and sacrifice. It carries with it responsibilities. A mother must teach, discipline, guide and nurture the young person to whom she gave the gift of life. When a child has been adopted, two people have played that special role in their life. It becomes an unexpected struggle when the birth mother becomes a conscious part of your life.

For nearly seventy years, the word, the title, Mother had exclusively identified Marguerite. She had done for me what every good mother does. And she had done this for the fifty years that we had together. Now, nearly twenty years after her death, I came to know another Mother in my life. This person had always been a mystery to me. Now, through the research I had done and meeting her daughter, Arlene, I have come to have an image of who she was. The person I had known only as Elizabeth was now taking on an identity. Known to her family and friends as Betty, she was the mother of my sister. She had had a family, a history and an ancestry. Stories of her life began to take shape and make Betty a real person in my mind. She was a person, over thirty years after her death, that I could love and respect. And I ache from her absence in my life.

From the moment we met, Arlene referred to her mother as "our mother." She had so generously shared her mother with me, and yet I found it difficult to refer to Elizabeth as my mother. I had a mother, who though she was no longer living, for whom I felt a fierce loyalty and love.

When I told Arlene of the problem I had with this, she suggested that my mother would always be my Mom, and her mother could be, Mother. That sounded good, but for one small problem. I never referred to my mother as Mom, neither when speaking to her nor speaking of her. As a small child, she was Mommy to me. When that stage was passed, I don't remember ever addressing her with a "title." When speaking directly to my mother, I started with the conversation, minus any form of address. In childhood, writing letters from summer sleep-away camp or from college, they were always begun with the salutation, "Dear Mother."

So how does one settle this unsettling dilemma? When speaking to my extended family, the word Mother, of course means their Aunt Marguerite. When I want to tell them something of Betty, I usually say "my other mother." But when I speak with Arlene and say "my mother" it seems wrong or awkward. In my mind I try to refer to "my mother" and "our mother," but it doesn't always flow that easily in conversation. This may seem like a trivial matter, but it is an important one to a person who is piecing together the puzzle of their life.

A further reflection on this quandary appears in a journal entry that I made on March 25, 2010. On that day I stopped at the cemetery to "talk" to my parents about the recent events of my life. My reflection on this visit goes like this:

> In the past 10 days I have celebrated, by recall, all of our birthdays. Tomorrow is the birth date of my "other mother, Betty." Earlier this month my sister,

Arlene, celebrated her Big 6-0. It just goes to show that all the best people were born in March!

As I stood, graveside, today, I could not help but notice the wording on the stones of John and Marguerite – FATHER and MOTHER. They selected as their identity, the relationship that I gave them. For the others in our family plot, although they were parents, that was not how they chose to be memorialized. There, chiseled in stone were the names

Peter H and His Wife Elizabeth

and his son,

Peter and His Wife, Catherine

But my parents chose to be remembered by the role they played in MY life.

I guess this struck me so hard because of my recent finding of my birth family. In a way I feel as though I have abandoned the ones who cared for, raised, educated and nurtured in Faith, this child they took into their hearts and home so unconditionally. I never doubted or questioned their love for me, but recently I question how well I showed my love for them in life and in death.

This has been an unexpected burden that accompanies the inexpressible joy in finding a sister and knowing more about my biological origin.

My Mother and Father will always be John and Marguerite. Their imprint is on my heart. May they rest in peace ~ a due reward for putting up with me!

Arlene and I have often questioned out loud and tried to plumb the depth of the mystery of whether or not my parents knew Betty or had any contact with her throughout the years. There was only one source of a possible answer to those questions. There was a woman with whom my mother shared the leadership of our Girl Scout troop many years ago. I can, so clearly, recall the evening when we were at a local department store. We met Mary there as she joyfully announced that she and her husband would be picking up their son on the following day. She was purchasing blue ribbon, to be incorporated into a little sweater set. Their long wait for a child to call their own would be transformed to reality the next day. Since she and my mother were good friends and they would share the sisterhood of being adoptive parents, I grasped at the thought that if my mother had known Betty, it may have been discussed with Mary.

Relaying this disappointing news to Arlene I said,

> *"I just got back from visiting with Mary - the one whom I had hoped might be able to shed a little light on why I was able to have the name and location of our Mother. She said she never heard my mother say anything about knowing "where I came from." She knew that they (my parents) had hoped for a second child, but were unable to get him. I knew about that, though. Peter was almost ours and I can even remember going to the Infant Home to meet him. But a childless family was also in the running and, since they had no children, they were chosen to make him their own. Mary said she can't remember how she knew that I was adopted, but she just sort of always knew it. She did say that she was aware of my adoption well before they adopted their 2 boys, so it wasn't a case of a*

"kindred spirit" thing. She and my mother were co-leaders of our Girl Scout troop for many years, so that's probably when the information was revealed. SORRY, no good leads to answers for the questions we have. But we had a nice visit."

The hope of having a clear answer to the question was dashed when Mary said that she did not recollect any conversation that would indicate that any contact had been made between my two mothers. This is a nagging question to which I would like to have an answer, but it seems, now, that I never will.

P In late March, Michael had notified us that Sarah had fallen and broken her hip, had surgery and was at a rehabilitation facility. He further stated that he would be coming from his home in Florida to see her. We took that news as a directive to make a trip to Hudson Falls to see Sarah and to have a visit with Mike. Though tired and in a fair amount of pain, she was very aware of our presence and entered in to the conversation in a limited but very lucid way.

Following our visit, Sarah was readmitted to the hospital the next day. She did not seem to be on the rapid road to recovery, as we had hoped. She did, however, return to the rehab center to go on with her healing.

Continuing our own tradition, on the Saturday before Mother's Day, Arlene and I made our now annual trip to Union Cemetery to honor our mother. As had also become our practice, we visited Sarah. Upon returning home, I reported to Mike.

Hi, Mike,

Arlene and I just got back from our trip up North.

We only stayed with your Mom for about 15 minutes.

She was asleep when we arrived. A nurse came in with her meds and woke her up. We identified ourselves and chatted for a few minutes and then she fell back to sleep. So we told her we were going to leave so she could rest.

The flowers you sent were on her stand. They are a beautiful Spring arrangement - bright and colorful.

It is way beyond beautiful here today. It was a good day to make the trip to Hudson Falls.

Take care.

Pat

On May 28 we each received word that Sarah had been returned to the hospital and that her condition was deteriorating. I knew in my heart what the likely outcome would be.

The day was bound to come. And now it has come and passed. On May 29, 2012 I received an e-mail message from Michael.

Hello,

I just wanted to let you know that my mother died this morning at 7:15 AM.

Mike

The news did not come as a shock. It came with the force of finality driving it.

When Michael's brief note arrived, it did not come as a surprise. Sarah was now free of the physical suffering she had endured over the past several years. The hip that wouldn't heal would no longer trouble her. The deep, abiding pain of shingles would no longer be an issue to be dealt with. She was at peace.

Standing before her casket with my sister, Arlene, at my side, a flood of emotions came over me. Here was the woman who made it possible for me to "know" my birth family. She it was who led me to my sister. Without her keen memory and willingness to share the missing piece of my life story, I would still be searching for answers. From the moment I met Sarah, five months after I began my correspondence with Michael, she shared my joy and shared her stories. The impact she had on my life cannot be measured. Nor is there a measuring device that could calculate the depth of my gratitude to her.

At her wake, Sarah's sons and their families were sharing stories from their childhood, recollecting the things they did as a family. These four men are now middle-aged and have had a lifetime to know and love and share their Mother. I have only known her for the last five years of her life. But in that short time, Sarah gave me a gift that only she could give. She gave me my history. She gave me a family to which I am bonded by blood.

My heart aches at the loss of Sarah. At the same time it rejoices that she came into my life and left an indelible mark. May she rest in peace.

In October, I was determined to continue the practice of visiting the cemetery for some time with my birth mother.

I invited Arlene to join me, but she chose to give me that time alone with our mother. Following a short time at her graveside, I journaled my thoughts.

Upon returning home, I wrote to Arlene.

P   *Hi, Arlene,*

I will send the "notes" when I get back to my laptop. As you may have noticed, I find it difficult to express some thoughts and feelings aloud. It comes much easier in writing. But, even at that, I am reluctant to share because I never figured anyone really cared that much. Too many times I have been criticized or challenged on what I have said about what I think or feel. So it's just easier to keep it to myself. But this is different. It's not that I think that I'm saying anything in a new or clever way. It's just documenting what is going on as I work my way through all the phases of this process. If it can be of help to someone it will have been worth the risk I take in sharing.

And YOU are such an integral part of this whole thing. I don't want to burden you with my emotional ups and downs and at the same time I don't want to leave you out of the loop.

    Pat

P   October 19, 2012 – Pouring Rain ! 35th Anniversary of Betty's Death – my sixth visit on this date.

For some reason, as I grieve the loss of one I never knew,

tears flow freely. The pain of loss deepens with each new realization of something I have missed.

Lately it is the fact that I never heard my mother's voice. Simple things I never heard her say: "How was school today?" "Come in. It's time for dinner." "Time for bed." "Good night."

I never heard my mother say, "I love you." Yet I know she loved and respected the little person that I was. I know this without a doubt by the heroic choice she made on my behalf. And again I thank her through my tears and sniffling. In the words of the poet, Francis Thompson, "Heaven and I wept together."

To this Arlene replied:

A *October 20, 2012*

Hi, Pat,

I read this earlier, but wasn't able to comment. It was extremely touching and I still cannot comment. Actually, I don't think a comment is necessary, nor should one be made. It was very moving and it brings up thoughts I have. Thoughts I will write out as well.

Arlene.

P   As wonderful as my life has been up to this point, it now has a dimension added to it that cannot be understood, save by someone who has not had the opportunity to know a "flesh and blood" relative for a lifetime and now has an honest to goodness SISTER.

A Over the past 4+ years, we have tried to not only "meld" our traditions but to come up with our own. It has been easy for me since, on the big holidays like Christmas, Thanksgiving, Easter, my husband and I have always done brunch. We remember, when our kids were young, having to make the rounds to my parents', his father's, his mother's, sometimes his uncle's. My parents eventually starting doing Christmas Eve celebrations and our Thanksgivings were moved from Thursday to Sunday, which is all well and good, but I guess I'm a bit selfish and still feel the need to have our holidays on the actual days. Therefore, we do brunch in the morning and everyone is free to go where they need to the rest of the day. As a result, it was pretty easy for Pat to begin joining us and still continue her own traditions with her family.

The pieces have all come together. The many pieces of our lives have been joined, interlocked forever, at last.

P **PostScript**: My only regret in this story is the fact that I never had the opportunity to tell, Betty, my Birth Mother how grateful I was for the choice she made on my behalf. Truly, she gave me the gift of life, twice.

A I also regret the fact that my mother never knew the gratitude Pat felt or knew what a wonderful person she grew up to be. I like to think she does now. I often wonder what would have happened if Pat had searched out her birth mother prior to 1977. How would my mother have reacted? Would she have been happy to be found? Would my mother have finally told me? Knowing my mother, she would have cried and told me we needed to talk. And what would my reaction have been? In the scenario I have in my head, the reason we stayed in Schenectady was so that, if Pat wanted to find her birth mother, she would be nearby. I guess it doesn't really matter, since that's not what happened, but I can't help but think, "What if...?"

All of the pieces came together when we met on

November 15, 2008.

This picture was taken on that occasion.

We have invited some of our friends and family members to contribute their observations on our wonderful story.

A Birth Mother Speaks

By Judy Loucks

Hi, my name is Judy and I am Arlene's sister-in-law (my husband, Chuck, is Arlene's husband's brother).

I came into this family of four brothers and three terrific sisters-in-law late in life. However, I was greeted and treated like I always belonged. I am an only child and now

I had a wonderful cadre of family, but the most supportive of all were Bruce and Arlene. We live in Florida and, for most of Chuck's and my 23 married years, they have visited us often and I was able to discuss things with them that I ordinarily wouldn't ever tell anyone, because I was ashamed. The shame and guilt of an illegitimate child carries out through life until finally someone, mostly yourself, tells you to stop. This is my story and I hope you will see how it correlates to Ar & Pat's.

When I was in my late teen years, I fell in love and, of course, became pregnant. As they say "in the day" this was totally frowned upon and completely unacceptable. There were two choices, a totally illegal abortion (very dangerous) or be hidden in disgrace from the rest of family and friends and eventually (for me anyway) to end up in a maternity home until giving birth. I was never, ever given the choice of keeping my baby. My Mother and Father made sure that I understood that my baby must be given up for adoption. For those of you who are young in today's world, you will never believe a mother could give up her child. But back then, there were no choices. I had grown up totally spoiled and didn't want to ruin the rest of my life because I had made such a shameful mistake (according to my parents and the times we lived in). There are a few funny asides - my mother and grandmother made my bounce down the stairs on my fanny day after day and my parents paid for very expensive horseback riding lessons in the hope I would miscarry. Oh well, too bad, so sad, for them, but wonderful for me to have had the experience of having a child, even if I couldn't keep her.

Happily, I gave birth to a beautiful little daughter whom I only got to see one time, but that memory will always remain with me. She looked exactly like pictures of me when I was born. I think of her every day, but that was 48 years ago. Hopefully, she is happy and healthy and has had a wonderful life. Because of Bruce and Ar, I did register with the foundation that tries to put parents and adopted children together, but nothing has ever come of that. The rules in those days were very stringent. A mother lost all claim to her child and the adoptive parents need never tell their child that he or she was adopted. Somehow I felt that comforting, because the laws were also very stringent about adoptive parents. They had to be perfectly upstanding, caring people who desperately wanted a child they could not have on their own. That is the main reason why I never pursued more vigorously my search for her in later years.

Now, the point of this story is obvious. Pat's Mom must have gone through a very similar situation. As a mother, you never forget about the child you have given birth to and totally wished and prayed to have her back. Times are so different now, but no one can imagine the shame heaped on you by family and friends and how you give in because of the pressure of guilt, which, by the way is totally unfair to all involved. But that was then and this is now.

One day Arlene called me and said "I am terrified". Now, just so you understand, Arlene is the perfect wife and mother (her daughters respect her as a mother, but also as their best friend). Her husband adores her. I asked her what in the world she could possibly be terrified about. She said "I am going to meet my real sister for the first time." When she explained the circumstances I told her she had nothing to worry about. If she was just herself everything would be fine. You all know the rest. When Ar called me back, she was in tears and astounded. She told me that Pat was amazing.

Arlene had lost her own mother at an early age and had a hole in her heart that she didn't even know was there. Then Pat appeared and that hole has been filled. I have met Pat on several occasions, and it is truly amazing how similar the two are, even growing up in separate situations. When they get together, they think and act like, well, sisters. Oh yeah, that's because they truly are and have found each other after years. So everyone, take heart, there are still miracles performed everyday.

These observations are from Arlene's daughters, Kristine and Gwen.

From Daughter, Gwen

When my mother called me one morning to tell me that she was contacted by a woman who claimed to be her half-sister I was shocked to say the least. We are the least controversial family I know. We have no family secrets, no skeletons in the closet, no drama. This news made me extremely nervous. Who was this woman? Would she be nice to my mother? Would she be bitter? Was she married? Did she have children? I had so many questions. This was the type of story I was familiar with only by watching Maury or Oprah. Those stories, more times than not, do not end well. I thought the odds were against us and I didn't want my mom to get her hopes up.

My mother and aunt scheduled their first meeting a couple of weeks after that first contact. I was more than a little bit afraid of what would happen. My mom is a wonderful person who wears her heart on her sleeve. I knew she wanted more than anything to become friends with her sister and I didn't want her to be hurt. My maternal grandparents both died very young and I have always felt sad that my mother did not have any family on her side still living. I wanted so much for them to hit it off.

Thankfully that first meeting went better than anyone could have expected. They became friends instantly. All of my worries were put to rest. My aunt is a strong, kind, smart and funny woman; we could not have asked for a better person to welcome into our family. When I met Pat for the first time I was struck by how much she looks like my grandmother, other than the fact that Pat is much, much taller. There is also a strong resemblance between my mother and Pat; for one, they have the exact same hands! They also have the same calm and friendly demeanor. I don't think I have ever seen Pat without a smile on her face.

I truly cannot be happier that my aunt found us. My only regret is that it didn't happen sooner. I love the friendship that my mom and aunt have. They are as close as two sisters that grew up together their whole lives. We are very lucky to have Pat in our lives.

From Daughter, Kristine

I remember the call like it was yesterday. It was 10:00 in the morning on a Saturday and it was my mom when I answered. She sounded a little nervous and I heard a shake in her voice. I thought it was maybe because she called me so "early". You see, a few weeks earlier I had asked that people not call me so darn *early* and set the time to 10:00am and not a minute earlier. Anyway, she said she needed to come over and show me something but wouldn't tell me over the phone. I was a little nervous but more excited to know what it was. As soon as she walked in she handed me a letter she got in the mail. Now I really had no idea what it could be. There were so many things running through my mind. I opened the letter and mostly skimmed it at first trying to get to the point as soon as possible. Then I came to the part that said "I think I might be your sister". Wait...what??? She actually waited until 10:00 on the dot to call me about this? I'm awful. So, I look at my mom, she looks at me with big eyes, I read the letter again, this time more carefully, then look at her again. She has tears. It's serious. Too serious. So I get nervous and say "she knows we don't have any money right?"

Ever since I was little I always wondered about my mom and her family. She had lost her mom, dad and brother at such a young age. What was that like? Did she miss them? Was it hard? She always had friends but that's nothing like family. I love my sister. I don't know what I would do without her. If we're not texting or emailing we're on the phone with each other pretty much all day, every day. I always wished my mom could have that too. So when she gets this letter that says she might have a sister...I couldn't have been happier or more excited for her.

The day my mom went to meet her at a restaurant it was so hard to let her go alone. I was going to sit in the parking lot just in case but she wouldn't let me. I mean...you never know right?? I walked around the house with my phone in my hand the whole time. I just couldn't wait to hear about it and I so badly didn't want my mom to be let down if it wasn't true. That would've been heartbreaking. So when she called I answered before the phone had even barely rung. Wow was she happy! Thank God!! She said she looked just like her mother. There was no question that they were sisters and I couldn't wait to meet her.

I don't really remember the first time I met my Aunt Pat. It was that easy. She came in one day and just....stayed. It's like she's been here all our lives. We definitely loved her right away. Her and my mom look alike. We had family pictures done and they sit exactly the same. They have the same hands! They're always on the phone or emailing each other or playing on-line games together, doing craft fairs, going out to lunch. It was an instant connection. I am so happy my mother finally gets to experience the unconditional love of a sister and it has truly changed her life in such a good and positive way. It really is my wish for my mother come true.

And by the way the 10:00am phone call rule no longer stands. So rude!

I love you both so much! :)

The next two contributors are sisters themselves. They are our mentors in being sisters. They are also our good friends. Their support and loving encouragement has been strongly instrumental in our putting this memoir on paper and making it available to those who might be thinking about embarking on a similar journey.

Sister/Friend

By Maryanne Tuite

Sisters are God's gift to those blessed enough to have one. Whether older or younger, right or wrong, they are in your corner – for life. Growing up from birth with a sister is unique to all relationships. There is always a history of stories, events, good times and bad times shared, however different from one's perspective!

Having my sister, Carolynn, in my life has been a distinct joy. She's everything a sister should be and sometimes I think we interchange older with younger and age doesn't exist. The roles meld. Sometimes she acts the 'older/wiser' and sometimes I do. It's a mutual give and take. We know what each likes and dislikes in food, clothing, perfumes, reading material and entertainment. Friends become 'our' friends yet distinct at times as well. There is a genuine deep caring and love that exists, expressed in a myriad of ways – respect, understanding, acceptance of each other's need for alone time and an expressed sensitivity to know when to say: 'let's eat out tonight'! One of our greatest gifts is our sense of humor – a gift given to us from our parents. It's gotten us through many a situation and as we've grown older in wisdom, age and hopefully grace, it's helped us to take ourselves less seriously. Our relationship is a bond that can never be undone. There's an old saying I once remember hearing, *'sisters are God's way of giving you a best friend for life.'* I know this to be true in Carolynn. It's wonderful not only to *have* her as my sister but to *be* her sister!

But what if one's 'sister relationship' doesn't begin until the second half of life? What if all those growing up experiences were only one dimensional? What shared stories are available to remember?

Someone once said: *'God seeks us out to give us to each other.'* With my good friend, Pat, and her sister, Arlene, that is just what God did! He knew both of them from the beginning and in His time placed them in each other's lives.

Pat and I met twenty years ago when we began our ministry as lay catechetical leaders in separate parishes. I learned over time that Pat is a gifted writer, a great organizer and a faithful friend. If you are blessed to have her in your life and you have no biological sister she *is* that sister! She has all the characteristics – she's present, shows up when needed, loves you unconditionally, laughs with you, cries with you, tells you the truth with kindness and doesn't expect you to be anyone except who you are! (Just like my sister, Carolynn!) Oh, and is always ready to have lunch with you – as is my sister as well!

So when her long, long search for her biological

Mother produced a *blood* sister I saw this as God's loving reward for all those whom she had 'sistered' over the years. Meeting Arlene has been a joy. She and Pat appear to have known each other all their lives as you watch their interaction. While they may not share growing up sibling memories they have had similar experiences which seem to parallel their lives. Being with them on this journey has been a privilege and a delight. I remember when my sister and I invited them for dinner to our home for the first time and Pat introduced her: *'This is my sister, Arlene! Arlene, these sisters are going to be our models for sistering!'* My sister and I looked at each other and said: *'Oh, boy, are they in trouble!'* Each had always wanted a sister and now God has brought them together and together they complete a part of their past. They are now sisters forever and friends always. I am honored to be a part of their present, part of their story and part of their lives.

What does it mean to be/have a sister
By Carolynn Tuite

Sisters – an unimaginable connection! Having been fortunate enough to have both parents in common, I have known my only sister since the day I was born. I knew she loved me from the get-go and I've always felt it through the years as it was nurtured, continued to grow and become deeper.

Are there things we do differently? Absolutely! Just ask any of our mutual friends and some even believe us to be polar opposites! But we had such a strong family bond in our younger years, a wonderful legacy from our father and mother, that we were destined to always be entwined in each other's life. That is something for which I will always be eternally grateful!

Perhaps there are some sisters that feel a sense of obligation to be there for the other but that's not how our relationship has made it through the years. Our emotional tie is probably greater since neither of us married or had a family of our own. We have always shown mutual respect for each other's life paths and indeed have encouraged and have been encouraged by the other to always move forward and follow our heart and strengths. I intuitively know that my sister can always be counted on to be there for me and will never stop caring about me. She is the one person who will never cease worrying about me and will always want the best for me.

We have been through a lot together through the years, the daring move from our hometown to a new city without the promise of a job and taking our 68 year old mom from her comfort zone to share this adventure with us! Buying our first home was wonderful experience for us. When our mom died at 86, we were there for each other. There were other lows, but I believe I've gotten through them because my sister has been there right by my side.

The good times have been great times and these far outnumber the difficult ones. We could not appreciate these without that kinship we share. The tears have been shed and shared only to have the laughter break through and move us forward. The ebb and flow of being a sister hopefully will continue many more years for us. I love having my sister and I can only hope I have been half as good at being one!

Being a friend of Pat first, I remember when she first told how this story unfolded and how she hesitated in approaching Arlene – taking months to send that initial letter! I'm not sure I would have had the courage to step off that cliff without knowing if someone would be there to catch you. But caught she was and by a wonderful, warm woman who accepted this new sister with open arms. What an incredible journey this has been for both of them and from my perspective, well worth every step they've made together. I'm thrilled to have been privy to witness the newfound joy that has come into their lives! I'm filled with excitement for them as they continue to discover things about each other in a short span of time. I'm convinced that finding a sister later in life offers many, many gifts that while different, are just as miraculous as having a lifelong sister. Wisdom does come with age. Receiving the gift of a sister at age 60+ offers unique points of view as well as a very deep appreciation for the life the other has lived. There may be some sadness thinking about a lifetime of family and memories that they were never able to share together due to circumstances beyond their control. But I feel that they are two strong, loving women who have started a joint life in total harmony and one that will endure for many, many years.

Watching Pat and Arlene build a relationship with a newly found sister has enriched my view of "sisterhood". This outside view certainly gave me a deeper appreciation for the common family history with my sister. I was thrilled when they told my sister and me that we were their mentor sisters. They watched us to learn how sisters acted toward each other! Yikes! What a responsibility! Yet, what a wonderful testament to our sisterly roles and I certainly hope we continue to set a good example for them but I actually think sometimes the roles are reversed. Whenever the four of us get together of course we share many laughs but much of the joy that fills the air emanates from Pat and Arlene. New sisters – new love! What a grand experience for all to see!

A testament to the mentoring occurred on a trip to visit our cousin, Sarah McCall, shortly after Christmas. We like to bring some small gift to Sarah when we visit her in the assisted living facility. Usually it is a plant or floral arrangement. We stopped at the Floral Department of our local market to make the purchase before heading North for our visit. Upon arriving home, it was with giddy excitement that I e-mailed Maryanne and Carolynn the following message.

> *I just want to report that your "mentoring" must be working. Arlene and I stopped to pick up flowers for our cousin in Glens Falls. As we were checking out, there was a little banter over how we'd pay for them. Each plant, on sale in this post-Christmas period, was 99 cents, so the grand total was $2.14 with the tax added. As we were discussing the high finances, the young (20ish) clerk asked if we were related. We sheepishly said, "Yes." And she replied, "You sound just like my sister and I."*
>
> *That was music to my (our) ears. Later on, it struck us funny that a woman her age would ask two much older women such a question. But we're glad she did.*

I asked a dear and long-time friend to share her observations of our experience. Although she has never met Arlene, she surely knows the impact she has had in my life. She truly shares our JOY.

Evidence of the great joy of sisterhood

By Maureen Cahill Organ

I had the good fortune to meet Pat for the second time somewhere around 1993 and I remembered her so fondly and so immediately.

The event was a reunion of counselors, other workers and campers who spent time at Marian Lodge. That was a camp for girls established in 1915 and relocated to Pyramid Lake in the Adirondacks of New York State in 1947. It is now a retreat center owned by the Catholic Diocese of Albany, NY called Pyramid Life Center.

I attended Marian Lodge as a camper starting when I was 7 years old. In 1958 Pat was a land activity counselor. It was so shocking that I knew her face so clearly from the moment I saw it after almost forty years. It was the recalled image of kindness. I absolutely remembered the patient and loving way that she interacted with the most vulnerable, lonesome and needy littlest campers. No wet sheets, interminable fits of crying or bad acting out behavior could separate her from loving the little children.

Over the years of the frequent reunions and a lot of joint work on projects, I have now come to know Pat in a peer-to-peer way and it has been a great treasure. I find her to be wise, very funny and caring and exquisitely moral. She is also very "private" and slow to share her innermost thoughts, especially of any emotional discomfort she might be experiencing.

Pat said very little about it during my mostly semi-annual contacts with her but I learned that she had lost three of her dearest and closest lifetime friends through death over a period of three years. It was obvious that these losses were a really heavy blow to her and that she was feeling somewhat adrift, sad and alone.

During our "work week" at camp in 2009 we had lunch at Pitkin's, our usual place to treat ourselves to a real meal in the town of Schroon as opposed to pick up light meals at the Center. (The Center was not yet opened for the season.) As soon as we sat down, she blurted out that she needed to tell me something. All I could think was, "oh shit, what has happened now?" Then I looked at her face and she had this most impish little grin that she could not contain and it burst all over her face in a nano-second.

She proceeded to tell me the abbreviated but fascinating version of her search for her mother, which included many intriguing facts of her life about which I had no clue. Of course she kept interrupting herself to announce in the capital letters that she is still using "I found MY SISTER."

The woman who had been adrift, sad and alone had completely vanished. She was full of joy and as exuberant as a pretty reserved person ever gets and she has remained that way about this relationship. Pat has a whole new lease on life and a whole new family to love her in addition to the great one she has had all of her life.

Pat and I continue to share many adventures that make us feel productive and fill us with fun. I know that Marian Lodge/Pyramid Life Center is really important to her in her core. I also know that there will never be a conflict for Pat between doing ANYTHING else and spending time with Arlene. SISTERHOOD reigns and I love seeing its effect. It's a bit like the giggling and all pervasive silliness that she sometimes shared and sometimes suffered through with us as little ones - way too much fun. It is a payback framed in justice for a great woman.

A Final Thought

It has been well over four years now, since the course of life changed dramatically for both of us. The newness has vanished like a morning fog lifts gently from the surface of a mountain lake. The reality is becoming somewhat akin to normal. The relationship we share still amazes us. But as the moments, days, weeks, months and now years pass, it is hard to imagine a time when we were not sisters. We fill in the blanks as best we can. We can now, in conversation, hark back to an event to which we were only present by proxy. There are times when I (Pat) find myself feeling a loss, perhaps even a sincere grief, for the years we did not have together. But at those times I also find myself appreciating more deeply the time we have together; treasuring every moment we share and looking forward to our next.

Resources for a Genealogy Search

If you are an adoptee, the quest for information can be daunting. As an adoptee, your age may be the key to the availability of information. The State in which you were born and/adopted will also figure heavily into the information that is available to you. All of this said, the following is a brief list of resources which may be of help to you. These will be of most help with adoptions within the United States. International adoptions have a completely different structure. The International Adoption Agency will have control of that information. In many cases, even they have little or no information about the birth parents.

Your Adoption Papers – do you have them? What information is contained in them? A LAST NAME is a good start.

Family Members – are a valuable resource. Ask your parents, aunts, uncles, life-long family friends what they can tell you about the time you were adopted.

www.Ancestry.com - is a service of the Church of Jesus Christ of Latter Day Saints (The Mormons). There is an annual membership fee for this site. It gives access to census records, military records, birth, death and marriages. It is extensive, very well indexed and easy to navigate.

City Directories – were printed by most cities prior to the advent of telephone books. They contain an alphabetical listing of the city's residents, their employment, and status as a home owner, renter or boarder. Most local libraries contain the City Directories for their locale.

Newspapers – on microfilm are available at most libraries and the state Library has them from most major cities dating back to the late 1800's. It can be tedious work, but obituary listings, births and deaths can be found in these papers. If, however, you were surrendered for adoption at birth, do not expect to find a birth announcement in these publications

School Yearbooks – from the major schools in the area can be found in local libraries. Smaller private schools may not have provided yearbooks to the library.

Cemeteries – You can often find whole families in one burial plot. Headstones will identify the relationship between the family members. In some cases, cemetery personnel will be helpful in locating burial sites within their cemetery. We have found that this is not always the case, but most usually is.

Churches - If you know, for example, where you were baptized, you can ask for a copy of your Baptismal Certificate. Know, though, that in the record book, there has been a notation made that an adoption has taken place and the only certificate they can issue is an "amended" one; it will not have the names of your birth parent(s).

State Adoption Registry - In New York State this is a repository of non-identifying information. How other states handle this type of information, I am not sure, but it is worth looking into. If it has been updated throughout the years, it can yield some valuable information. There are states which have kept the adoption files open and the information you are seeking may be available for the asking. For a fee, in New York State, you can register to be contacted if your birth parent or a sibling also files a request. It can be a long shot, but you may want to take the risk.

The Adoption Agency – should have your records on file. How much information they are free to share will depend on the policy of the agency and the regulations of the individual state.

Time, Patience, Perseverance – will be your greatest asset in your search for information. No clue is too small to be considered significant. The pieces of your puzzle will not be given to you in logical order. You may travel down many dead-end paths before you find a useful piece to add to your puzzle.

A Word of Caution – Finding a birth parent or a child you relinquished for adoption may not have the outcome for which you had hoped. Tread lightly. Be sensitive to the position of the birthmother and the burden she carries. To be combative, angry, confrontational or demanding can only have a painful outcome for all concerned.

Remember to enjoy the journey.

Made in the USA
Middletown, DE
03 March 2019